A Short History
∽ of the ∽
Wellington Boot

A Short
the Wellin

Adam

History of
gton Boot

Edwards

HODDER &
STOUGHTON

Copyright © 2006 by Adam Edwards

First published in Great Britain in 2006 by Hodder & Stoughton
A division of Hodder Headline

The right of Adam Edwards to be identified as the
Author of the Work has been asserted by him in accordance
with the Copyright, Designs and Patents Act 1988.

A Hodder & Stoughton Book

1

A CIP catalogue record for this title is available from the British Library

ISBN 978 0 340 92138 8
ISBN 0 340 92138 2

Picture acknowledgements
The Advertising Archive: chapter openers 9,10; Bridgeman Art Library: 4, 5, 6;
Corbis: 7, 9, 11, 14, p. 100; English Heritage/Nigel Corrie: 2; Getty Images: 8, 10,
12, 13, 15; Heritage Image Partnership: 3; Mary Evans Picture Library: 1, p. 16.

Typeset in Goudy Old Style by Hewer Text UK Ltd, Edinburgh
Printed and bound by Clays Ltd, St Ives plc

Hodder Headline's policy is to use papers that are natural,
renewable and recyclable products and made from wood grown in
sustainable forests. The logging and manufacturing processes are expected
to conform to the environmental regulations of the country of origin.

Hodder & Stoughton Ltd
A division of Hodder Headline
338 Euston Road
London NW1 3BH

Contents

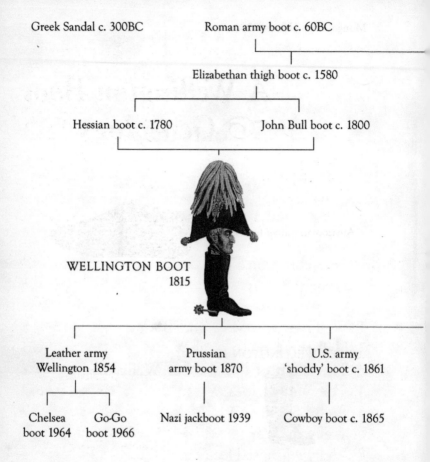

Greek Sandal c. 300BC   Roman army boot c. 60BC

Elizabethan thigh boot c. 1580

Hessian boot c. 1780   John Bull boot c. 1800

WELLINGTON BOOT
1815

Leather army   Prussian   U.S. army
Wellington 1854   army boot 1870   'shoddy' boot c. 1861

Chelsea   Go-Go   Nazi jackboot 1939   Cowboy boot c. 1865
boot 1964   boot 1966

Mongol High Heels c. 1200

A *Wellington Boot*
∽ Genealogy ∽

Amazonian rubber boot c. 1500

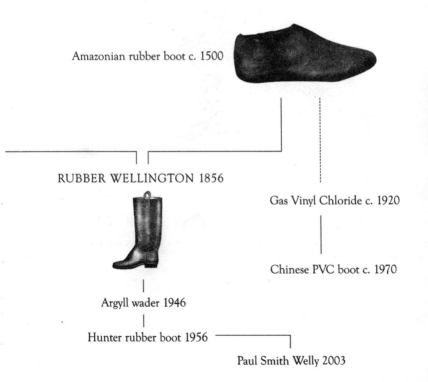

RUBBER WELLINGTON 1856

Gas Vinyl Chloride c. 1920

Chinese PVC boot c. 1970

Argyll wader 1946

Hunter rubber boot 1956

Paul Smith Welly 2003

Preface

A Yorkshire country museum—
The Duke's Valet—The Welly boot grail.

John Spencer, curator of the Duke of Wellington's Regimental Museum, is not army. No, sir. The middle-aged chap in charge of the military collection looks more like a beaten-up survivor from a late Sixties American West Coast rock band than an old soldier. His long, lank, salt-and-pepper hair hangs to the waist of his baggy blue jeans, held up by what looks like an American Civil War belt with matching ammunition pouch.

We are standing in front of a dim glass case in the former drawing-room of Banksfield Mansion, a blackened Italianate pile on the outskirts of

Halifax. The memorabilia in the cabinet belongs to the 1st and 2nd Battalions of the Duke of Wellington's Regiment (West Riding) and is displayed in this neck of Yorkshire because this was where the Iron Duke's soldiers were recruited.

Spencer pulls on a pair of white rubber gloves and unlocks the case. Then he bends down in the gloom and searches by the base of a tailor's dummy clad in nineteenth-century regimental dress uniform. When he straightens up he is holding a tatty boot in either latex-clad hand.

They are short black calf boots – about size six – with neat, swan-necked, steel-wheeled spurs built into the back of the low heels. The soles are thin and the leather uppers scuffed and torn. In places the stitching is beginning to come apart, and the wooden 'boot-trees' cannot be removed in case the whole thing falls to pieces.

The old boots arrived at the museum by a circuitous route. It inherited them from the former United Services Museum that had originally been given them by Captain Gilpin of the 84th Regiment in the late nineteenth century. Gilpin had got the boots from a friend of James Hall, a lawyer and amateur portrait painter living in Soho's Brewer Street. Hall had in turn acquired them from Christopher Collins, the former valet to Arthur Wellesley, the first Duke of Wellington.

According to Wellesley family tradition the valet inherits the uniform of his master, and when the old Duke died in 1852 Collins snaffled the lot. He had subsequently given, or more probably sold, the footwear to James Hall, who was in the process of painting a posthumous portrait of the legendary field marshal.

With the boots came a note. It read, 'Sir, the enclosed is some more of the Duke of Wellington's old things which I promised you I would let you have, and I can assure you that they are the same as his Grace left them of [sic]. Your Humble Servant, Christopher Collins.'

Here, in the 21st century, held up by a one-time hippie standing in the middle of a Victorian pile, is the Welly boot grail. What might look to some like a dull piece of regimental kit of no more interest than a cap badge or webbing belt is in fact an artefact of overwhelming international importance. These plain black leather boots, invented by the first Duke of Wellington and the only pair in existence known to have been worn by him, are the prototype of the boots that were to conquer the known and unknown worlds. Here in Halifax, languishing anonymously in an unlit display case, is the original of one of Britain's greatest icons – the Wellington boot.

1

Wellington – Man and Boot

The Duke's funeral described—The Welly's place in the cortège—The Welly as national icon—Marie Celeste and Paddington Bear—The Welly in literature and art— Its influence on world affairs.

On 18 November 1852, Arthur Wellesley, first Duke of Wellington, was laid to rest beneath the dome of St Paul's Cathedral in a ceremony that was one of the most spectacular events this country has ever seen. The Iron Duke had lain in state in Chelsea Hospital for two days while tens of thousands of people filed past the coffin. The crowds were so great that two of them were crushed to death.

And then, on the morning of the eighteenth, his body was taken from Apsley House, his Hyde Park Corner home that boasts the address

'Number 1, London', in a vast procession which slowly passed through the streets of the city. It travelled along Horse Guards, the Strand and Fleet Street and ultimately to the West End door of the cathedral. A million men and women lined the route to watch the twelve-ton funeral carriage followed by the Duke's riderless horse. In the stirrups of the horse's saddle, placed the reverse way round, were a pair of the Duke's hand-made Hoby Wellington boots.

An early Wellington boot from the North British Rubber Co. (now Hunter's)

Wellington – Man and Boot

It was a measure of the Wellington boots' importance that the footwear was given first place behind the hearse, ahead of the score of regiments, the dozen marching bands and the important mourners who included foreign dignitaries and senior politicians from across the globe.

It was in many ways the leather Welly's greatest day. The empty boots were a catalyst that engendered an outpouring of emotion that was not to be seen again until Princess Diana's funeral. Never again would a single item of dress reduce a nation to tears.

And the boots have continued to hold their place in the country's heart, moving from the sublime to the ridiculous. The rubber Wellington, the direct descendant of that day's funereal centrepiece, remains a source of patriotic pride and national amusement. In the British it brings out both the sensible and the silly. It is as much part of our make-up as a morning constitutional or a *Carry On* film.

The writers of *Monty Python's Flying Circus*

understood the importance of the Wellington
boot in the nation's psyche and highlighted
the fact with the creation of the 'Gumbies', a
race of characters who are loud and stupid with
knotted handkerchiefs on their heads and 'gumboots' (hence the name) on their feet. All the
Pythons played Gumbies, usually standing together in a row in rolled-up trousers, braces
and Fair Isle sweaters with fists clenched and
arms held down in front of them shouting like
daft yokels. But it is their Wellingtons that we
remember. The Welly represents the Pythons and
therefore us. The rubber boot has come to sym-
bolise the drollery of our nation.

And yet the boot is more than a collective
laugh. The Wellington boot has helped find the
man responsible for perpetuating the hoax of the
Piltdown Man – the apparent discovery in Sussex
in 1908 of the missing link between man and ape.
The mysterious 'gentleman in black' who was
supposed to have arranged the fake bones was
seen wearing Wellington boots. It was therefore
correctly assumed the hoax must have been

organised by local man Samuel Woodhead as 'no gentleman before the Great War would have travelled from London in Wellington Boots'.

It was also the Wellington boot that was responsible for the final discovery of the fabled ghost ship the *Marie Celeste* that had been found sailing off the Azores in 1872 without a soul on board, the captain, his wife, their two-year-old daughter and the entire crew having vanished. The ship continued to sail under a different name under different owners for another twelve years. Her last captain loaded her with a cargo of rubber Wellingtons and then deliberately scuttled the vessel by running her on to Rochelois Reef in Haiti. Afterwards he filled in an exorbitant insurance claim for an exotic cargo that never existed, forgetting that its actual cargo of boots would prevent the ship from sinking. Insurance investigators inspected the wreck and on discovery of the boots brought proceedings against the captain and the first mate, who were later convicted on charges of barratry (fraudulent practices by the master of a ship).

The Wellington boot has been an inspiration to great artists and musicians. Charles Dickens wrote about it in *The Pickwick Papers*, while *Nicholas Nickleby* contains the following description of Ralph Nickleby: 'He wore a bottle-green spencer over a blue coat; a white waistcoat, grey mixture pantaloons, and Wellington boots drawn over them.' The boots are central to the work of many painters from Winslow Homer (in his painting *Prisoners from the Front*) to the Sixties pop artist Allen Jones.

Wellingtons are prominent in Moncrieff's opera *Giovanni in London* and also appear in the work of Sir W. S. Gilbert. In *More Bab Ballads* the operetta composer who collaborated so successfully with Sir Arthur Sullivan writes of 'two shirts and a sock and a vest of jean, a Wellington boot and a bamboo cane . . .' The American singer/songwriter Paul Simon dedicated a song to the boots on his album *Graceland*, and jazz giant Edward Kennedy 'Duke' Ellington was given his nickname because his refined manners were reminiscent of the booted Duke of Wellington.

The musical *Gumboots* is based on the trials and tribulations of South Africa's black miners and their Wellingtons. The oppressed men, forbidden to talk to each other and frequently held below ground for three months at a time, gradually developed a system of communication by stomping and slapping their Wellies. It was the Wellington that was the vital ingredient in *The Great Welly Boot Show*, from which emerged a group of Scottish comedians including Billy Connolly, the Glaswegian wit who subsequently created 'The Welly Boot Song'. And it has contributed to the success of many British sitcoms, from *Last of the Summer Wine* to *The Fall and Rise of Reginald Perrin* (in which his boss CJ remarked ironically, 'I didn't get where I am today by going on and on about gumboots').

It is safe to assume that Paddington Bear would not be the bear he is today without his red Wellies, despite the fact that he didn't wear them until 1972 when the first soft toys of the character were produced. (A television production company attached them to the furry figure at the last moment because the standard model Paddington was unable to stand up without them.) And where would Winnie the Pooh's chum Christopher Robin be without his boots?

The *Dandy*'s anti-hero Desperate Dan wore Wellingtons. The long-running *Daily Mirror* strip 'The Perishers' has an anti-hero called Wellington who not only wears the boots but has an old English sheepdog called Boot. And 'Wonder Wellies' in *Buster* magazine had boots worn by the character Willie that could fly off, scoop things up and stretch themselves to disproportionate lengths.

The Wellington has been the centrepiece at the fetish ball in London's Soho (*The Deviant's Dictionary* defines the love of the Welly boot as 'retifism'). The gay scene celebrates the boots with a website dedicated to the workingman's Wellington, while Dutch boot fans dress up in their favourite Wellies for a sexual buzz. The world of pornography in general would be considerably poorer without the boots. *Welly Girls*, for example, is the third in a series of films featuring 'sensational lesbian Welly Boot action, with the girls doing just about whatever they like to each other'.

At fêtes and church fairs across Britain the sport of Welly Wanging – chucking a single boot as far as possible – is practised during the summer. The Scotch Malt Whisky Society lovingly describes its cask number 41.29 as 'the colour of golden syrup with the scent of the inside of a Welly boot', while Beatles' Wellingtons were imported to America during the heyday of the Fab Four.

Today the boot remains at the forefront of rock and roll and high fashion. Model Kate Moss is pictured looking chic in Wellington boots at the Glastonbury Festival, and Pete Doherty from Babyshambles signs a boot at the Reading Festival that is subsequently auctioned for the charity Children in Need.

Meanwhile a visit to any football ground in Britain is not only an education in British history (the Union flag is celebrated, the language is Anglo-Saxon and the chants recount victories from Waterloo to World War II) but a chance to shout, 'Give it some Welly!'

But to laud the Wellington boot as no more than a fun national symbol would be to do it a grave injustice. The boot has changed history. It has crossed every river, marsh and wetland of every country on earth to help build and maintain the British Empire. It has been intrinsic to the South America rubber boom and essential in building the New World in North America. It was vital to the Allied victory in the Second World War, helped in the development of Asia and played an important part in the emancipation of women.

It is a boot that has been worn by the highest – kings, queens, dukes and Diana Spencer at Balmoral when the Prince of Wales was courting her – and the lowest. It is, as those million souls who watched the late Duke's cortège could never have guessed, the unsung hero of the last two centuries.

2

Hail the Conquering Welly

*Arthur Wellesley, Duke of Wellington and inventor of
the boot—Its ancient ancestors—The Hoby Wellington—
George 'Beau' Brummell adopts the boot –
Praise from* Punch*—The Queen's joke.*

Arthur Wellesley, the first Duke of Wellington, was born in Dublin in 1769, four
months before Napoleon Bonaparte. He
was the son of a viscount, who purchased a
commission for him in the British army on his
eighteenth birthday. He rose quickly through the
ranks and served in both Europe and in India
before assuming command of the British army in
Portugal in the Peninsular War against Napoleon.
The battles of the Napoleonic Wars culminated in
1815 in Wellesley's and the country's most cele-
brated victory – Waterloo.

In recognition of his achievement he was raised

to the peerage as the Duke of Wellington. He sat in the House of Lords for the rest of his life, while remaining Commander-in-Chief of the British Army, and was active in politics including a brief stint as Prime Minister. But ironically it was his leather boot, which would evolve into the rubber Welly, that was to become his lasting legacy.

Victory at Waterloo would turn Wellington into a charismatic cross between Winston Churchill and Lady Diana Spencer. He was a

THE WATERLOO COCK WOT'S LOST HIS COURAGE

An 1832 cartoon showing Wellington as the 'Waterloo Cock'

warrior with a dress sense, a sword-wielding David Beckham, who had conquered Europe with cannon and was now about to do the same with his boot.

Until that victory it had been the French who were renowned for their sartorial *savoir-faire* and, under Louis XIV and his successors, it had been France that had dominated European fashions. But after the Revolution and Napoleon's eventual defeat at Waterloo the continental look became as dated as a droopy musketeer's moustache. Now it was the Iron Duke who would set the fashion agenda. It was his boot that would be worn in the capitals of Europe.

Wellesley's Wellington evolved from the warrior's boot that had been worn for thousands of years. Ancient Greeks had had boots that fitted snugly around the calf with the toes exposed, while the Romans' calf-length military boots had hobnailed soles in which the copper nails were replaced by gold and silver when the soldiers returned home. Mongol tribesman added their two ingots to boot history when they invaded

Europe on horseback sporting bright red high heels.

The Elizabethan thigh boot – which was as important as the codpiece to the military – remained a favourite for Charles I, who had suffered from rickets as a child. He hid his temporary affliction from the public with concealed brass supports in the heel and at the ankles of his boots. When he became an adult, and was able to walk without the help of supports, he continued to wear boots out of preference. After the Civil War his wrinkled cavalier's boot was stiffened and straightened into a more austere piece of footwear.

And as civilisation and culture took hold in the eighteenth century the black boot was relegated to the military, for riding and outdoor living. The high-heeled, buckled winkle-picker was the preferred indoor wear.

Ironically, it was the introduction of pavements that brought the boot back into fashion. Eighteenth-century London and county towns had begun to pave their squalid streets, which meant that the gentry were now able to walk to where they wished instead of taking a carriage or sedan chair. For this reason the top boot of the sort caricatured by John Bull began to be popular, and by the start of the Napoleonic Wars it had made a complete return to high fashion. In Jacques-Louis David's famous painting *The First Consul crossing the Alps at the Grand-Saint-Bernard Pass* Napoleon Bonaparte is pictured wearing just such a pair of John Bull boots with the tops turned down.

Wellington too wore boots. His boot of choice was the knee-high soft leather 'Hessian' boot from Germany. The Hessian was an under-the-knee boot with a V-cut in the front from which a tassel frequently hung. It was named after the state of Hesse and had been introduced in England in the late eighteenth century by the immigrant German *demi-monde* imitating the military footwear of the Hessian soldiers. Young Englishmen copied the Hun and also wore a shorter version of the Hessian, the popular Hussar Bushkin boot.

And then came Waterloo. Wellington returned the conquering hero, surrounded and fawned on by the fashionable set while the populace followed and copied his every move. It was in this climate that the great soldier asked his shoemaker, Hoby of St James, to modify his Hessian boot, to make a boot that he could call his own. He did not want a boot that he wore outside his trousers. He did not want a boot with continental connections or one that harked back to the previous century. He wanted an English boot that could stand proud anywhere in the known world.

The result was the Wellington. It was a plain boot with no decorative stitching, in black leather with side seams, one-inch stacked straight heels, square or slightly rounded toes, and leather pull-on straps. It was worn under trousers with a strap under the instep.

The Duke took to wearing his boot around the capital. It was as admired and copied as a Manolo Blahnik, in particular by the most famous fashion victim of the day, 'Beau' Brummell.

George Bryan Brummell, wit, dandy and best friend of the first Duke of Wellington, was born in

1778, the son of the private secretary of George III's Prime Minister, Lord North. After Eton College, where he was known as 'Buck', he joined the Prince Regent's regiment the 10th Hussars, a company famous for its dressy uniform. And it was while serving with the Hussars that he became a close companion of the future George IV and Wellington.

Beau Brummel took his toilet and clothes very seriously. He did not enjoy, for example, the overpowering foetid smell of body odour that, along with a variety of crude fragrances, tended to emanate from your average late-eighteenth-century male. He bathed every day and insisted a gentleman should smell of clean linen and country air. Nor did he like powdered wigs, make-up, beauty spots, coats of silks and satin, knee breeches, silk stockings and coloured high-heel shoes.

When it came to dress, Beau was a puritan. He eschewed the flamboyant coat of its day with its trendy peacock colours in favour of a well-tailored black wool jacket, and instead of the chopped trouser he adopted the pantaloon (a nineteenth-century variation of ski pants). It had straps across the bottom of the foot that kept the trouser legs tight and so allowed the young blade to wear them under a pair of new highly polished patent leather Wellington boots.

It took Brummell five hours to dress. He had three hairdressers to groom him, one for the sideburns, one for the forelock and one for the back of the head. He had two glove-makers, one of whom made only the thumbs of the gloves. And he was the first man to starch his cravats, which he sent to the country when they needed cleaning and starching, as he claimed it was only in the backwoods that they knew how to bleach.

But most of all he was a fusspot about his boots, a garment which had by the early nineteenth century risen from the barracks to the ballroom. Lord Byron, a close friend of the fop, wrote that there was nothing really exceptional about Brummell's dress 'save a certain exquisite propriety'. That propriety included a pair of brilliant boots copied from the Duke's original Hoby pair. And once Beau wore them the court followed suit. A courtier without a hand-made Hoby pair of Wellington boots was as worthless as a fop without a limp wrist. The leather Welly was to Regency England what the deck shoe is to Blair's Britain. It was the unspoken mark of the well-to-do. And every day Beau's valet would polish his master's boots with champagne to keep them looking a shade sharper than his contemporaries' footwear. He buffed the uppers and the soles with the sparkling French wine until even the edges shone like mirrors.

Two years after Waterloo the Wellington boot made its first appearance in a Northampton shoe-maker's factory list costing one pound five shillings (£63.50 in today's money). By 1830 they were available in London's first shoe shop, Alfred Carter's Wholesale and Boot Warehouse, for only a guinea a pair. It was indicative of the boot's popularity. Everyone wanted a pair, not just those who could afford to buy bespoke, and the prices reflected this.

There were other boots available at the time.

Blüchers, which looked a bit like the Second World War British army boot, were named after the then very popular Gebhard Leberecht von Blücher, the Prussian field marshal who fought alongside Wellington at Waterloo. But his boots were no match for the Wellington.

Its popularity was now so great that not only did those with a well-turned foot sport it, but also anybody who needed a practical boot copied it. They included those who rode or marched and, in particular, those who had to walk any sort of distance, including the first thousand of Sir Robert Peel's new-fangled policemen.

The 'Peelers' wore a top hat commonly referred to as a 'stovepipe', a dark blue swallow-tailed coat (in the tails of which was a truncheon) and Wellies. Each Peeler patrolled his beat at a pace of two and a half miles per hour. He walked on average twenty miles a day, in all weather conditions, seven days a week.

The only way to achieve this feat successfully was to wear the boots that were designed by Robert Peel's greatest friend the first Duke of

Wellington. It was the Wellington boot that enabled the 'bobby' to pound the beat. It was the Welly that came running at the sound of the police whistle, that stamped its authority on the criminal underclass, that patrolled the cities and made them safe for the new industrialised gentry. And it is why the first Duke, with remarkable understatement, described the new force clad in its uniform of Wellington boots as 'very respectable'.

At that time, the Duke could still occasionally be seen in Hessian boots. But the satirical art of William Heath, who drew under the pseudonym of Paul Pry, finally put an end to that. Despite the fact that Heath's sharply observed etchings of the Duke and other senior government figures were beginning to be frowned upon by the emerging puritanical Victorian society, his 1830 portrait of the Duke's head poking from a Wellington boot achieved national recognition. After that caricature the Duke would only wear boots of his own design.

That same year *The Whole Art of Dress* was

published. It claimed that 'the Hessian' had lost its position in the fashion stakes and was 'now only worn with tight pantaloons'. The top boot too, it said, had become merely a sporting fashion 'although they are worn by noblemen and gentlemen in hunting and they are in general use among the lower orders such as jockey, grooms, butlers'. Wellingtons, on the other hand, were now 'the only boot in general wear'.

In 1841 the satirical magazine *Punch*, also known as *The London Charivari*, ran an article in praise of the boot. 'Boots? Boots! Yes, Boots. We can write upon boots – we can moralise upon boots; we can convert them into a thousand similes,' it stated. And it proceeded to do so. The magazine embarked on a lengthy piece on the matter of the fashionable footwear of the day. The thrust of the feature was that while the entire population wore boots only one was worthy of the mid-nineteenth-century dandy's foot – the Welly.

There were other types of boot that could be bought off the shelf, but none, it stated, matched the brilliance of the boot that had been created and popularised by the Duke. It described the Blücher as a cut-down Wellington that had 'no right to be made at all'. Blücher boots, it claimed, were 'decidedly ugly commodities, chiefly worn by purveyors of cat meat and burly-looking prize-fighters. They are eight-and-six-penny worth of discomfort. One might as well shove one's foot into a box-iron.'

Ankle-Jacks, similar to Blüchers but rising up above the ankle, fared no better. 'They thrive chiefly in the neighbourhoods of Houndsditch, Whitechapel, and Billingsgate and attach them-selves principally to butchers' boys and itinerant purveyors of "live fish",' *Punch* reported.

Hessian boots, worn outside the trouser, were 'little more than ambitious Wellingtons. They are curved at the top, wrinkled at the bottom with a tassel in the front,' it sneered. 'And they are fast falling into decay. Like dogs they have had their day.'

Punch also complained about the old 'top boot', which, after a brief foray into fashion with John

Bull half a century earlier, had returned as the sole preserve of those who rode. The boot needed to be made-to-measure, to be 'lasted, back-strapped, top'd, wrinkled and bottomed'. The magazine dismissed them as designed for 'little Frankensteins' (jockeys) and said that they should only be worn as a sporting fashion 'by stable lads or hunting gentlemen'.

Unequivocal praise was reserved for the Wellington, in particular for a pair that had been crafted by Wellington's boot maker, Hoby of St James. 'Wellingtons are perfect as a whole; from the binding at the top to the finish at the toe, there is a beautiful unity about their well-conceived proportions,' said *Punch*. 'The boots are kindly considerate of the calf, amiably inclined to the instep, and devotedly serviceable to the whole foot. They shed their protecting influence over all they encase. They not only protect the feet but honour the wearer.'

Four years later James Develin, writing in *The Shoemaker, The Guide to the Trade*, Volume 2, claimed that the English were now 'a booted people'. And just as *Punch* had earlier heaped praise on the Wellington boot, so too did he laud its infinite variety. 'Some have green legs, some purple, some yellow, some are made of black Spanish leather and some of white grain calf, some of a sort of half and half mixture,' he said. 'But all are magnificent.'

That was the year the term Welly entered the language. An entry in the ledger of London boot maker Dulton and Thorowgood dated 25 February 1845 reads: 'Master Oldship, a pair of Welly bt cloth front.' Two months later another entry refers to '1 pr. of light calf Welly boots'.

By now the Wellington boot had become so dominant that in 1848 the popular *Lady Book* complained, 'For half-a-century men have adhered formerly to the heavy, clumsy and unnecessarily expensive Wellington.' The writer advocated the elastic-sided ankle boot, which was said to be cheaper and lighter.

Shortly before the Duke of Wellington's death Queen Victoria asked the great man what type of boots he was wearing. 'People call them Wellingtons, Ma'am,' he said. 'How absurd,' replied the Queen. 'Where, I should like to know, would they find *a pair* of Wellingtons?' It was an excellent joke, for while the Duke was unique the answer to her question was 'everywhere'.

3

The Birth of the Rubber Welly

*Columbus's rubber ball—The amphibian Amazonian
rubber boot—Macintosh's melting coat—Hancock's
pickling machine—The race for the patent—
The Wellington's fate hangs in the balance.*

I n 1853 the first Duke of Wellington died and
in the years immediately after his death his
finest creation, the leather Wellington, began to fade from high fashion with the carriage
crowd. It was the elastic-sided ankle boot rather
than the Wellington that clicked above the late
Duke as he lay in his massive sarcophagus in the
crypt of St Paul's Cathedral.

And yet even as it began to disappear from the
London store windows it was to be reborn in
another guise thanks to the new material bub-
bling from the trees the other side of the Atlantic.

Rubber had been found in South America. Its

discovery would give the leather Welly its scion, a rubber boot that would take up the footwear flame and would come to change the industrialised landscape.

The first rubber artefact created by man was probably the rubber ball. The South American Olmec tribe, whose name means rubber people, is credited with the actual invention of the round toy.

Rubber aficionados claim that it was Christopher Columbus's visit to Haiti on his second American voyage that discovered the globe-shaped amusement for the West. He sailed back to Portugal in the *Santa Maria* with the rubber ball that he would subsequently use to demonstrate that the world was round.

What was more important was that in 1615 Fray Juan de Torquemada published *Monarchía Indiana*, a description of pre-conquest Mexico based on sixteenth-century texts, which saw rubber move from ball to boot. Torquemada describes how the native Indians not only waterproofed capes by dipping them in the juice of the rubber tree but also made a similarly fashioned boot. 'The Amazonian native,' he wrote, 'protects his feet by dipping them into latex to produce a perfect fitting pair of galoshes.'

It was the amphibian rubber boot's first appearance to the awed visitors from the Old World. The waterproof boot, they knew, was easily as important a find as tobacco or the potato.

Forty years later Father Bernabe Cobo's *History of the New World* talks of 'coating long stockings with latex to protect legs when walking in the jungle', while reports from Mexico claimed that the Spanish court conducting the Inquisition there amused itself by giving hunchbacks joke rubber shoes to make them fall over.

In the eighteenth century the French astronomer Charles Marie de la Condamine joined an expedition to Peru and sent rubber home to the Académie Royale des Sciences with an accompanying report stating that the natives were making shoes from it. 'The boots are waterproof and when smoked they have the appearance of leather,' he said.

A Short History of the Wellington Boot

Rubber artefacts from the Amazon basin

[34]

The name of the tree from which the milk or 'latex' flowed, he said, was *heve*, and the name given to the material by the Indians was *caoutchouc*, meaning 'the tree that weeps'.

Another Frenchman, François Fresneau, wrote a paper on the natural rubber boot, in which he gave details of its native manufacture. 'Coat a clay-mould with latex, dry it over a smoky fire and then crush the clay and remove it through the neck,' he wrote. It is the first known description of the manufacture of a gumboot.

Fresneau died in 1770, but his work had raised rubber from a passing curiosity to a possibly useful raw material. His death coincided with Joseph Priestley's observation that, in the artists' materials shop Nairne's of London, 'One could buy half-inch cubes of material from Peru for three shillings that could be used for erasing pencil marks.' Priestley, the scientist who discovered oxygen and laid down the foundations for modern chemistry, christened the object 'India Rubber' because it came from the Indies and rubbed out. Sixty years later the expression had become part of the language. Charles Dickens wrote in *The Pickwick Papers* that the lines on Mr Pickwick's brow melted away 'like the marks of a black lead pencil beneath the softening influence of India Rubber'. It would be another fifty years before scientists started using that term instead of the clumsy 'caoutchouc', which is still the French for rubber.

Despite this seemingly universal enthusiasm for the new substance no one knew how to stop it clotting once it had been bled from the rubber tree. By the time it arrived in Europe the liquid rubber had transformed itself into solid matter which was hopeless for any sort of experimentation. Scientists instead turned their attention to finding a solvent.

It was Glasgow chemist Charles Macintosh who discovered that ammonia turned the coagulated block of rubber into a solution. Macintosh painted his mixture on to two different sides of fabric and pressed the pair together. The result was the raincoat, which he started producing in 1823 and immodestly christened the Macintosh.

In its early days, however, his 'Mac' wasn't much good in either the cold of the winter or the heat of the summer as the rubber solution in the material became rock hard in chilly weather and turned into gum under a blazing sun.

On the other side of the Atlantic, American merchantmen sailing between Brazil and New England were also struggling with the solidifying juice. They carried lumps of it as ballast and dumped it on the wharves at Boston. Meanwhile above deck the most popular Amazonian trinket brought back by the sailors was the latex shoe.

'One of the shipmasters exhibited to his friends ashore a pair of native rubber shoes fancifully gilded,' reads a report in the *Boston Gazette* of 1825. It was a rarity as most rubber shoes were thick, heavy, unadorned objects. Yet, despite those inelegant drawbacks, within a few years half a million pairs were being imported annually from the Amazon basin. This continued until, thanks to Macintosh's ammonia, New England manufacturers began to bid against one another for the gum – which had hitherto been used only

A Short History of the Wellington Boot

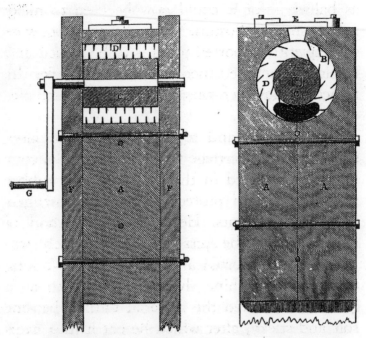

A A, two pieces of wood bolted together.
B, a hollow cylinder cut out of A A, and studded with teeth.
C, a cylinder of wood studded with teeth, and having a spindle passed
  through it.
D, space between the two cylinders B and C.
E, an opening with a cover.
F F, two pieces of wood bolted on both sides of A A, and enclosing the
  space D, and cylinder C.
G, a winch.
The darkened spot in space D represents the charge of rubber.

Hancock's pickle

as ballast – for it could now be used to make rubber shoes in Boston. Many of these shoes were subsequently exported to Paris to be 'gilded and fashioned' and returned to the States. Like the raincoats, however, they were useless in extremes of heat and cold.

As New England togged itself out in latex shoes, London carriage maker Thomas Hancock became interested in the possibilities of rubber as a material to protect his coach passengers from the elements. He devised a method of amalgamating the scrap pieces – which was how it was imported at the time – by working them in a machine that he referred to as a 'pickle'. It worked the material until it became soft and sticky, after which he cut it into strips and moulded it. He experimented with gloves, braces, garters and, in particular, the soles of shoes.

Unfortunately Hancock's rubber footwear, with its cloth and velvet uppers, suffered the Macintosh fate – they were not much good in extremes of weather. But that was soon to change thanks to the work of a humble Connecticut hardware shop owner – Charles Goodyear.

Goodyear was perpetually struggling to make ends meet. In order to pay off his debts he would try to come up with money making ideas. In the summer of 1834, while browsing at the Roxbury India Rubber Company, America's first rubber manufacturing company selling rubber footwear and rubber life jackets, he came to the conclusion that he could invent a better valve for the 'life-saver'. He bought a life jacket, but by the time he had got it home he had lost interest in the valve and fallen in love with its fabric.

'There is no other inert substance that so excites the imagination,' he later wrote in the first volume of his forbiddingly titled autobiography, *Gum Elastic: its Applications and Uses*. In the limited edition 1855 book, published between thick black embossed rubber covers, he writes about the first few pairs of side-opening 'native gum elastic shoes', known more commonly as 'India Rubber Bottles', that had been brought back by the Boston sailors a quarter of a century earlier. 'At that time their uncouth and clumsy shapes added to their weight, which was a great hindrance to their introduction: notwithstanding which, their importation continues to increase,' he wrote.

Goodyear, who according to one of his neighbours cut a ludicrous figure in his 'India rubber cap, stock, coat, vest, shoes and India rubber purse without a cent in it', dreamed of inventing the perfect waterproof shoe. He was determined to manufacture a rubber boot that was light, elegant and flexible.

He first experimented with magnesia to make the rubber stable, but it sagged into shapeless lumps. He tried to tame the material with a score of different chemicals, but none worked until he accidentally spilled nitric acid on to the rubber and discovered that this made it smooth and no longer sticky.

It was, he thought, his 'Eureka' moment, and he won a government contract to make rubber mailbags. But the New England summer that year was unnaturally hot and by the time the bags were ready for delivery the sun had returned them to gum.

It was back to the drawing board. Or, as Goodyear puts it in his book, 'the inventor made some experiments to ascertain the effect of heat upon the same compound'.

In fact the melting mailbags were his real breakthrough. Goodyear, who always wrote in the third person, started burning rubber. 'A specimen being carelessly brought in contact with a hot stove charred like leather. He [Goodyear] however directly inferred that if the process of charring could be stopped at the right point it might divest the gum of its adhesiveness throughout which would make it better than the native gum.'

Charles Goodyear had invented vulcanised rubber. It was to give the world the rubber Wellington boot. He called it 'metallic gum elastic' and patented it.

Vulcanisation made rubber both supple and hard. It was described in ecstatic terms in American newspapers as 'elastic metal'. The hard ebonite was immediately put to use in hundreds of objects from military epaulets to umbrella handles. The material was so revolutionary that women even took to wearing it as jewellery. According to the 1891 book *Industrial Curiosities* its prettiest application was when it was made to look like jet.

Shortly before Goodyear took out his patent he had shown the vulcanised rubber to a shoemaker friend called Horace Cutler. The two men set up a business in Connecticut to manufacture rubber overshoes and boots, and as the shoes improved, so did their popularity. The public snapped them up and soon the company was producing fifteen thousand pairs a day.

It was the success Goodyear had dreamed of, and he devotes an entire chapter of his autobiography to his rubber shoes, which he said had 'a perfection of finish and a style of execution, which is hardly surpassed in any branch of manufacture'. His factory could barely keep up with demand, it was doubling production every year and huge numbers were being exported to England.

'The boots are now to many persons, an article of absolute necessity,' wrote Goodyear. 'Their great economy is a great temptation, especially for the labouring classes to wear them constantly. They are equally comfortable or more so than shoes made of cloth or leather, so far as relates to the upper portion of them.'

Furthermore the footwear was cheap. Even in the early days of its manufacture 'gum elastic' or, as it was sometimes called, 'vegetable leather' was cheaper than animal leather. 'The future usefulness and extent of this branch of gum-elastic manufacture can hardly, at the present day, be estimated,' he wrote.

He was right. Goodyear's vulcanised rubber turned the shoe industry on its head and led, ultimately, to the creation of the British rubber Welly.

In England Thomas Hancock was still pickling. In 1825 he was granted a patent for the manufacture of rubberised cloth and by 1837 he had teamed up with Charles Macintosh and invented the spreading machine for coating fabric with rubber. During those years the Hancock and Macintosh partnership used elasticised rubber in almost every piece of clothing from stocking tops to braces, stays and waistcoat backs. It was used for pocket openings (for those worried by pickpockets) and wigs (to keep them on) – and to a certain extent for crude shoes.

And it was during these years that Hancock perfected his pickling machine. He had developed it into a power-driven tool designed to tear and masticate the rubber. It was so powerful and menacing that the name it was given, and the name that was stamped in large steel letters on to its main frame, was 'Iron Duke'. Poor Hancock had no idea that the name was a foretaste of the Welly future.

In 1843, while openly admitting that he had seen samples of Goodyear's 'cured rubber', Hancock obtained an English patent for 'vulcanisation' (William Brockendon, who also worked with Charles Macintosh, gave the process its name, saying, 'The mythical God of fire Vulcan would be familiar with both heat and sulphur.') It later transpired that Hancock had beaten Goodyear to the vulcanisation patent by eight weeks.

The transatlantic rivalry between the two men intensified. Hancock claimed the credit for the discovery of vulcanisation and replied to Goodyear's scribblings with a book of his own entitled, almost as forbiddingly, *The Origin and Progress of the Caoutchouc or India Rubber Manufacture in England*. In it he asserted that it was he who produced 'trouser straps, vest back straps, swimming belts etc. etc.' and, in particular, rubber shoes at least ten years before Goodyear.

Furthermore he claimed that his rubber shoes were far superior 'in lightness and elasticity' to Goodyear's American footwear, although he had to admit that his shoes had 'very little shine or gloss upon them'. Unfortunately the public preferred the polished American product and shipments from the States of Goodyear's shiny vulcanised rubber overshoes far outsold Hancock and Macintosh's rubber footwear in the UK.

The two partners were furious. The imported shoes could break the company and it went to court to claim the American shoe infringed Hancock's copyright. Not surprisingly the English court agreed and Macintosh and Hancock won the exclusive rights to produce the vulcanised shoe in Britain. This incensed the American shoe trade. It claimed that Hancock had stolen Goodyear's idea and that the British inventor should provide evidence for the work that he had done on his patent. The result was another court case, in which Hancock again won.

Hancock was the victor and vulcanised rubber was about to become as important to Britain as coal, cotton and steel. In the twenty years since Hancock had invented his machine for rubberising cloth, imports to the UK of raw rubber had risen from less than a hundred tons to over two thousand – half the output of the Amazon basin. However, Hancock had won the battle, but not the war. The destiny of the rubber Wellington and control over its production still hung in the balance between Britain and the United States.

4

The Welly Goes West

The Wellington's fall from favour at home—Its exile in the New World—Marching through Georgia in shoddy boots— A Wellington boot fit for cowboys—Its Hollywood career.

The rubber Wellington boot began to emerge into civilisation just as its leather parent was beginning to drop out of fashion. By the 1860s the leather Welly was no longer a sign of status on London's streets. It was seen as a military boot. Officers from all regiments, and in particular the cavalry regiments, wore them. But while police and army embraced it the fashionable had dropped it. The benefits of rubber vulcanisation had included the improvement of elastic. Elastic-sided shoes were the rage, and the calf-length, all-leather Welly looked less chic on the streets of the capital than a platform boot on a punk.

But despite its new status as fashion victim the leather Wellington did not die – instead it went into exile.

During the heyday of the leather Wellington, the Yankee bootmaker S.C. Shive had patented the patterns and crimping board for an American Wellington boot. His boot was an almost exact copy of the bespoke Hoby boot whose design the Duke of Wellington had commissioned in 1815. And just as the Peelers in London thought the Welly the perfect boot for the job, so the American cowboy and his military counterpart found it suited their needs. Furthermore its low-cut heels and calf-high uppers made it easy to mass-produce, and with the arrival of Civil War in 1861 it became ubiquitous.

The Wellington boot was the uniform of both sides. It would have been as celebrated in the States as the Colt 45 and the cowboy hat, had it not been for unscrupulous civilian contractors, who made the majority of military boots, supplying both Yankee and Confederate armies with cheap versions. It was reported at the time that a

considerable number of the US army's Wellington boots were made from reinforced cardboard.
This is despite the fact that military experts still
argue that victory by the Yankees was in a large
part due to the superior footwear of the Union
Army.

By the end of the war the soldiers who left for
civvy street to become cowboys, ranch-hands,
lawmen and gunslingers walked away from battle
in whatever they had been wearing – and that
was mostly clapped-out Wellington boots. Early
photographs taken just after the Civil War show
groups of cowboys all wearing Wellingtons. The
tops were either cut straight across or curved
slightly higher in the front.

'The Wellington was the basic utilitarian footwear that sprang from British influence and im-
migration,' says Tyler Beard in his definitive work
on the cowboy boot, *Art of the Boot*.

But cheap manufacturers during the Civil War
had debased the boot that had proudly crossed
the Atlantic only two decades earlier. The Wellington may have fought on both sides, but in

doing so it gained an unfair reputation. The boot was known as 'shoddy'. This terrible slur on the Welly was used to describe its rotten state of repair. The word had originally been applied to the cheap woollen cloth made from mill sweepings that fell apart as soon as it got wet. But by the end of the war it was being most commonly used as a derogatory term for the second-rate army-issue boots.

When the war ended the federal government had half a million pairs of 'shoddy' Wellington boots surplus to requirements. It should have dumped them. Instead over the following years it continued to issue them to its victorious Union Army, which soon discovered that the footwear fell apart in the tough climate and terrain of the Wild West that it now patrolled.

The fault lay not in design, but in manufacture. Yet those bad boots created the start of a boot trade. Civilian cobblers, mostly British immigrants, were at first forced to repair the dilapidated military issue. But eventually new boots were needed. And the cobblers, remembering the old country and the proud heritage of the boots, modelled the new boot on the old army-issue Wellington.

This is why the Wild West's greatest heroes such as Buffalo Bill Cody and Wild Bill Hickock are always pictured wearing classic leather Wellington boots.

In 1870 boot maker John Cubine, from Coffeyville, Kansas, added his own ugly variation to the boot. He made the heel higher – and cut it in at an angle – and embellished the front with a piece of cut-out leather. The Wellingtons he made for his Texan clients, for example, had a five-point Lone Star inlaid in the centre of the upper. This vulgar 'piecing' of the front of the Welly quickly became the distinguishing characteristic of the non-military boot. Cubine's final insult was to change the name of the boot. He called his bastardised Wellington boot the 'Coffeyville' boot. It is this so-called Coffeyville boot that experts claim has subsequently been copied, modified and occasionally embellished to emerge as the modern cowboy boot we recognise today.

And yet it is in truth modelled on the tall-topped Wellington boot designed by the first Duke and should still be known as such.

Kansas boot maker Dean Hyer of C. H. Hyer and Sons, which was founded in 1874 and is one of the oldest surviving boot makers, confirms this view. 'In the 1870s, almost everyone still rode a horse, so it would not be uncommon at all for the US Marshals, stage drivers, gamblers, prospectors, and common townspeople to be buying tall-topped boots,' he says.

This is perfectly illustrated by the leather Wellington boots worn by Henry Fonda in his seminal role as the bad hat in Sergio Leone's immaculately researched epic *Once Upon a Time in the West*.

John Cubine and his Coffeyville boot must take a deal of the responsibility for the general ignorance nowadays about the part the Wellington boot played in the making of America. But, as is so often the case, Hollywood too must take some of the blame. It is the silver screen that metamorphosed the cowboy boot from its actual roots as a Welly to its flashy Western look.

'Cowboy boots rose to a fashion high as a by-product of the entertainment industry's success with the cowboy hero,' writes Tyler Beard in *Art of the Boot*.

Early cowboy films were made in the eastern states of America. The filmmakers based the boots of their heroes on the exaggerated clothing seen on the covers of penny and dime novels. The fictional comic-cuts characters wore Wellington boots that were prettified and had little to do with corralling cattle, chasing Red Indians and conquering great tracts of the western United States.

It was only when the industry moved to California in 1914 and employed real cowboys as extras that the filmmakers realised that cowboys had not worn fancy comic boots at all but the basic leather Wellington. But by then it was too late for the Wellington boot to receive the plaudits it deserved. Like today's celebrities, the highly paid actors of the time revelled in their star status and continued to insist on wearing the absurd decorated boots outside their trousers.

Cowboy boots were no longer for protection against rattlesnakes, cacti and saddle sores or for holding up a pair of spurs. They were in the limelight, and the more garish the better. The Wellington boot had been tricked out and turned into a celebrity.

With its new flashy looks, the boot's career in the spotlight continued with the cowboy entertainers at rodeos. The brighter the boot, the easier it was to be seen from the grandstands. And the popular new cowboy crooners such as Gene Autry, Roy Rogers and Dale Evans aped the rodeo boots. They, along with the new Nashville country music scene, took the Welly on its final turn into mass-market American footwear.

Within twenty years the bastardised Wellington boot had become a fashion classic. And by 1980 the movie *Urban Cowboy*, starring John Travolta, had turned it into urban chic.

Only now is the backlash starting. The cowboy

boot is returning to its roots. It has come full circle and cowboy boot makers like D.W. Frommer have begun to produce the proper nineteenth-century cowboy boot.

Frommer's catalogue boasts of 'a two-piece boot, with the whole front, from the toe to the knee, being one piece and the whole back, from the heel to the calf, also one piece'. This is, the company claims, the boot that was worn by Civil War officers and the historical antecedent of the cowboy boot. Frommer has correctly named it 'The Full Wellington'.

Or to put it another way it was the Welly that won the West.

5

Welly Salad Days

An American entrepreneur in Scotland—The rubber Wellington unveiled—The rubber boom and bust—An undercover mission—The Welly boot zips up.

Thomas Hancock's brilliance in beating the Yanks to the British patent of vulcanised rubber had a major weakness – the inventor had failed to notice that it related solely to England rather than the whole of the United Kingdom. (Until 1952 it was necessary to apply for patents separately in England, Scotland and Ireland.)

The American entrepreneur Henry Lee Norris soon realised Hancock's dreadful mistake. Norris registered his own trademark and the Goodyear patents in Scotland. In the early 1850s he arrived in search of a suitable site north of Hadrian's Wall to produce rubber footwear. The sharp-witted businessman, 'a man half of Puritan and half of Lowland Scots stock', had been a rubber merchant in New York who had established a rubber manufacturing business in Brazil and had even briefly been the American consul in Para (now Belém). Now he decided that he would manufacture boots in Scotland rather than the States for the same reason that a century later Granada Television would chose to broadcast from Manchester rather than London. Just as Granada in its innocence believed that wet weather was needed to encourage people to stay at home and watch TV, a hundred years earlier Norris believed that the endless Caledonian rain would mean more customers for his boots.

He established the North British Rubber Company in a block of buildings known as Castle Silk Mills in Edinburgh in September 1856. And as no Scot had the faintest idea how to make rubber boots he imported four skilled workers from New York, three of whom were women. The descendants of these North American artisans may claim they were the producers of the first rubber Wellington boot – but the boot itself was made in Scotland.

In the years before the emergence of that 1856 Wellington from the North British Rubber Company, rubber shoes and boots were unbelievably crude compared to the highly sophisticated bespoke leather Wellington boot. Rubber footwear was made on straight lasts with no difference between the right and left shoe and only two widths, slim and stout, of which the latter was achieved by putting a pad of leather over the last. But the arrival of the Welly fired the shoemaking industry into a flurry of activity.

Until the 1850s all shoes were made with the same hand tools – a curved awl, a knife and a scraper – that had been used in every century in every country since the Egyptian sandal in the fourteenth century BC. Only pliers and a hammer had arrived to update the cobbler's collection. Early nineteenth-century efforts to industrialise shoe production had failed. The best anyone could come up with was a machine to compact the fragments of sole leather, which was introduced in America in the 1840s.

The breakthrough came in 1846 when American inventor Elias Howes unveiled his sewing-machine. A decade later his compatriot Isaac Singer introduced his universal commercial machine. And when news of the new rubber Wellington boot reached him, his competitive streak immediately turned to improving production of the leather shoe. With the help of one of his employees, a machine overseer in his shoe factory called Lyman Reed Blake, he adapted one of his machines to sew soles of shoes to uppers.

This machine led to arguments between skilled and unskilled labour. Exhibitions were staged across the entire shoe industry to demonstrate that machines could not compete with skilled craftsmen, some of whom were producing stitching so fine that they needed to use needles made from a single human hair.

It was while this row raged that the North British Rubber Company was establishing itself as the foremost rubber boot maker in the world.

Soon other companies rushed to catch up with it, and the first of them, established in 1859, was the Liverpool Rubber Company (later acquired by Dunlop), that began manufacturing under licence from Goodyear's bitter rival Thomas Hancock. Both companies began by making a raft of rubber goods that had become possible and practical since vulcanisation. Hats, coats, capes, cart sheets, horse cloths, umbrellas, waterproof tents, cushions, dinghies – the list was pretty near endless. It ranged from the useful galosh to the less useful 'greyhound stocking' for 'protecting the elegant creatures' toes'. But most particularly the two companies were rivals in the production of Welly boots.

Charles Goodyear, who in his 1855 book on 'gum elastic' devoted pages to discussion of the types of footwear that he had created from vulcanised rubber, was fanatical about the rubber boot. 'Vulcanised gum elastic boots are comfortable enough to be worn at all times,' he wrote. 'They are made by covering a felt boot with a sheet of elastic compound on the outside. These boots have been highly approved to be worn for a day in severe cold or stormy weather. When thus worn, or for standing or for wading in water or snow-water in cold climates, they are unquestionably more comfortable than any other boot.'

The emergence in the Scottish capital of a vulcanised Wellington boot modelled on the first Duke's design shook the rubber world. Suddenly an industry that had been in its infancy was now a player on the world stage. American companies like Goodrich, Tew & Company and The Boston Woven Hose & Rubber Company began to compete in making Wellington boots, overshoes and galoshes known colloquially as 'rubbers'. In Europe, in addition to the big two, others such as Harburg & Vienna Rubber and Hutchinson of Paris began producing boots.

It produced a rush for the new wonder material that would in turn create turmoil in the Amazon basin, open up south-east Asia and ultimately result in the invention of the zip. For very soon Welly boot producers diversified and began to use the raw material for literally hundreds of other applications, from seals for sewers to conveyer belts for steam engines and springs for railway rolling stock. The simple rubber Wellington boot had started a stampede.

The rush for the material in South America was comparable to the San Franciscan gold rush a few years earlier. By now it was clear that the best rubber for boots came from the wild Para tree (*Hevea Brasiliensis*), which grew exclusively in the land to the south of the River Amazon.

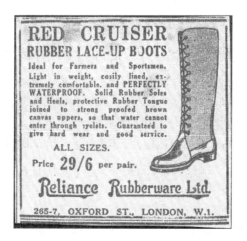

The red cruiser, a model long since discontinued

It was the place for adventurers, for shady businessmen and young blades and for those of a scientific bent. One of these was naval officer Clements Markham, who was devoting the equivalent of his gap year to journeying around Peru. There he made two important totally unrelated discoveries that would have a huge effect on the industrialised world in the coming decades. The first discovery was that a tree called the Cinchona produced quinine. His second, more prosaic one was that the wild Para trees were dying from over-tapping. All rubber supplies were dependent upon the collection of rubber from these wild trees growing in the Amazon basin (and to a limited extent upon the *Funtumia elastica* tree growing in the Congo). Markham realised there was no control of the raw material. It was collected and processed under primitive conditions, with little organisation; the trees were being badly damaged and the native labourers were abused.

Markham was determined that the supply of rubber for Britain's Wellington boots would not be subject to the vagaries of an untrained and ignorant labour force over which his own country had no control. He returned to England, joined the Civil Service and made it his first job to organise the movement of the Cinchona tree to India and south-east Asia. There the quinine produced by its bark would be used for the treatment of tropical diseases and, what was almost as important, for the creation of the tonic water that would accompany the Bombay gin drunk by the English bosses who would run his planned rubber plantations.

During his frequent journeying back and forth from Peru and India with his Cinchona trees, Markham wrote to the India Office suggesting the establishment of the Amazonian Para tree in south-east Asia, across the subcontinent and in particular in Ceylon (now Sri Lanka).

'When it is considered that every steam vessel afloat, every train and every factory on shore employing steam power must now of necessity use India rubber, it is hardly possible to overrate the importance of securing a permanent supply in connection with the industry of the world,' he wrote. The need for rubber for the Wellington boot went without saying. In 1873 he contacted the director of Kew Gardens, Sir Joseph Hooker, and asked him to arrange for Para rubber tree seeds to be sent to Britain. Hooker in turn asked the adventurer Sir Henry Wickham, who was in the Para State in Northern Brazil, to collect as many seeds as he could at ten pounds a thousand.

During the first six months of 1876 Wickham collected 70,000 seeds and personally shipped them back to Kew. When the Brazilian government discovered their loss it described Wickham's action as 'despicable' and condemned him as a thief (while in England the man who assured the future of the Wellington boot was given a knighthood). Brazil swiftly introduced a massive export tax on seeds and eventually followed it up with a complete ban on any seeds leaving the country – but it was too late.

Of the thousands of seeds sent to the Royal Botanic Gardens 2,397 germinated. Most went to Ceylon, where 90 per cent survived; the rest were shipped on to Singapore and Malaysia.

At first the transfer of the seeds did not much affect Brazil. Its rubber was still the main source of Britain's Wellies. And the country continued to boom in the years immediately after 1888, helped by the Scottish veterinarian John Boyd Dunlop, who had invented the pneumatic rubber tyre after seeing his son struggle to ride a tricycle over cobblestones. This new demand for tyres in addition to the need for rubber for boots sent the industry into overdrive. There emerged an army of rubber barons in Brazil, building palaces, running private armies, slave-trading and trans-acting business in gold coins. The Brazilian town of Manaus, for example, having started life as a small Portuguese garrison town, became over-night the richest city anywhere in the Americas.

The remote jungle town, which even today is only accessible by water or air, had streetlights and trams before most of Europe. So wealthy were its citizens that they would give vintage wine to their horses, edge their Wellies in gold thread and send shirts to be laundered in Lisbon. The town even built itself a magnificent neo-classical opera house, the 670-seat Teatro Amazonas immortalised in Werner Herzog's film *Fitzcarraldo* about an Irishman who dreams of Caruso performing in the jungle. Construction of the theatre began in 1882 and it opened with a gala performance on New Year's Eve in 1896 and dazzled for a few glorious years.

But soon after the turn of the century the rubber seeds smuggled out to Kew began to destroy Brazil's economy. It was South America's greatest financial disaster – the equivalent of its South Sea Bubble. (The scale of the country's ruin can be gauged by the rise of the Malayan rubber industry. In 1898 there were two thousand acres of plantations in the south-east Asian province; twenty years later there were over two million.) The city of Manaus was literally plunged into darkness, with no money to import coal for the generators. The rubber barons went back to Europe, while the opera house was left to rot in the tropical heat. Brazil never forgave the British.

Wickham too had fallen out of favour by the time of his death in 1928. Henry Ridley, the director of Singapore Botanical Gardens, re-marked, 'I looked on him as a failed planter. He was lucky that for merely travelling home with a lot of seeds he received a knighthood and enough money to live comfortably into old age. He was jolly well paid for a little job.'

But this was a slur on the saviour of the Wellington. The seeds he smuggled out of Brazil formed the basis for all today's plantations in the Far East and are still referred to as the 'Wickham' seeds. And the rubber created from those seeds was to become as important to Britain and the rest of the civilised world at the turn of the twentieth century as silicone was to become a hundred years later. And just as Silicone Valley bristled with start-up companies climbing on the back of the early Internet, so it was with the new rubber companies such as Goodyear, Firestone and Michelin that rode on the wave created by the Wellington boot.

Michael French, in his treatise *The Growth and Relative Decline of the North British Rubber Company*, claims: 'Firms diversified into general rubber goods in response to demand and in order to capitalise on their technical expertise.' He adds that it was the Wellington boot that had been 'the great strength'. And the Wellington boot was still riding high when the Brazilian rubber industry tumbled.

'This has been an exceptional year in respect of the designs in rubber footwear,' noted *India Rubber World* magazine in October 1900. The star of that year was the reinforced 'Royal Oak' Wellington that 'prevented the boot breaking out at the side or wearing out the toe'. Another success was the 'New Wales Goodyear Rolled Edge Armour Clad Boot' whose name, according to the magazine, 'suggests pretty fully the character of the goods to which it is applied'. And there was the Apsley 'Washstand' boot, a light boot designed for grooms cleaning carriages.

In Paris the fashionable were providing Wellington boots for their dogs after the New York millionaire Nathan Schwab had ordered a bespoke set of four bootees for his dachshund.

'It is the proper caper in Paris to provide foot-

1. Engraving of Wellington by Charles Turner, 1806.

2. Wellington's boots, on display at Apsley House.

3. Wellington's funeral carriage, 1852

4. *The Whittling Boy* by Winslow Homer, 1873.

5. *Napoleon as First Consul Crossing the Alps at the Grand Saint Bernard Pass* by Jacques Louis David, 1801.

6. Colour lithograph of Beau Brummel.

7. Hitler and state officials, 1937.

8. Landgirls hoeing in Evesham.

9. Inspection of boots belonging to the Manchester Fire Service, 1939.

10. Five ages of the Wellington boot. From left to right, 1896, 1914, 1916, 1925 and 1928.

11. Charles and Diana in the country, 1981.

12. The Queen in casual dress at Windsor, 2002

13. Mary Quant wet weather wear
including wet look boots, 1963.

14. Kate Moss in wellies
at the 2005 Glastonbury
Festival.

15. Boots left outside the entrance to Thames Television studios,
following an appeal for Namibia refugees to help prevent
foot infections from hookworms, 1978.

wear for dogs,' reported *India Rubber World*. 'Any high toned pup whose owner fails to furnish storm shoes is not keeping up with the procession.' The buttoned boots started at twelve francs and came with matching rubber storm blanket and collar.

In Britain, in the summer of 1903, the *Westminster Gazette* reported: 'The rage for rubber still increases. First we put it on our bicycles, then on our carriages and now on our feet. There is no doubt that a rubber boot is an excellent institution and those who have worn it once wear it always. Not only does it give an elasticity to the tread that reminds one of holidays and walking on the Downs but one is no longer worried about the steady clomp clomp of one's own feet on the paving stones. If everybody wore rubber what a different place London would be. And the life of the London worker would not only be quieter and more restful but it would probably be longer.' And in conclusion the newspaper praised the rubber sole and heel for 'saving the late church-goer from attracting inconvenient attention should the aisles be paved with tiles'.

The Wellington was now so popular on both sides of the Atlantic that it was used as the vehicle to launch the latest wonder invention – the zip.

Chicago mechanical engineer Whitcomb Judson, who had already invented a railroad braking system and the street car, hit upon the idea for opening and closing the Welly when he saw a friend with a bad back having trouble bending over to pull on his boots. Judson found a way for his chum to fasten them using only one hand with his patent 'Clasp Locker' or 'Hookless Fastener'. It consisted of a pair of small chains of alternating hook-and-eye locks and a metal slider that joined the two. He sewed them to his rubber boots and set out to market it from a booth at the 1893 Chicago World's Fair celebrating the 400th anniversary of Christopher Columbus's discovery of America. Twenty million people attended the 65,000 exhibits that included the first Ferris wheel, the first elevated electric railway and a movable pavement. The clasp sold just twenty, all to the US Postal Service for mailbags. Unfortunately the result was similar to Goodyear's dealings with the mail service fifty years earlier – unmitigated failure. His clasp locker jammed, rusted and was difficult to use.

Judson died before he could perfect it. But his death did not stop other inventors trying to find a way to open and close the Welly. In 1912 Swedish-American engineer Otto Frederick Gideon Sundback invented the 'Hookless Number 1'; a year later he came out with the 'Hookless Number 2' and followed that up with the 'Separable Fastener' in 1917. Six years later Benjamin Franklin Goodrich, the man who now ran the most successful rubber company in the country, ordered 150,000 separable fasteners for his rubber boots. While listening to the sound created by the device, Goodrich came up with the word 'zipper', a name that unfortunately he failed to trademark.

In the 1940s the zipper, which had been conceived as a side closure for Wellies, overtook buttons as the main form of closure for men's trousers. *Esquire* magazine declared the zipper-fly

A Short History of the Wellington Boot

The zipper – invented thanks to the Wellington

[76]

the newest tailoring idea for men. It would, it said excitedly, 'exclude the possibility of unintentional and embarrassing disarray'. The article was head-lined 'The Battle of the Fly'. It is not a fight that Wellington, the great warrior and inventor of the boot, could have imagined.

6

Welly at War

*Florence Nightingale and the Wellington—Barefoot in
Sebastopol—The leather boot of the officer class—
The rubber boot in the trenches—
The Welly makes a Christmas Truce.*

Throughout most of the nineteenth century and some way into the twentieth,
the Wellington boot symbolised the British army. The boot, like the red coat, was a
metaphor for the ordinary soldier fighting the
nineteenth-century colonial wars to keep Britain
great. Because of its association with the Duke of
Wellington, it was seen as the country's guardian.
The armed forces embraced it and made it an
integral part of their uniform.

In the Crimean War (1853–56) the Light Brigade wore it for the fateful charge on the
25 October 1854, and it was the 93rd Foot's boot

of choice when the regiment was christened the 'thin red line' after its battle with the Russian cavalry.

After the battle of Inkerman, however, in which the British and French armies successfully withstood an attack by the Imperial Russian army, the Welly would play a very different role – by a twist of fate, its absence would lead to a revolution.

Following the battle a huge storm wrecked 21 Allied vessels sitting at anchor in Balaclava Harbour, including the merchantman *The Prince*, a screw-driven ship with a crew of 150 that was driven broadside on to the rocks after slipping its single stream-anchor. Fewer than ten of her crew survived, and her entire cargo of forty thousand Wellington boots was lost.

Without boots many of the British troops spent the rest of the campaign with their feet wrapped in cloth. Some wore boots borrowed from dead Russians; others had gaiters made from old knapsacks and leggings made from sheepskin and buffalo and horse hides.

When new Wellingtons did arrive from Britain, Lord Raglan, commander of the British Army of the East, complained that they were 'far too small and extremely ill-made'. Pairs issued to the 55th Regiment, for example, frequently had their soles pulled from them when the men started to march through mud. That in turn led to dreadful foot ailments, including hundreds of cases of frostbite. Elizabeth Davis, a tough Welsh medical officer, who was working with Florence Nightingale at Scutari, the barracks hospital where the pioneering English nurse earned her reputation after Inkerman, wrote: 'I shall never forget the sights as long as I live. I began to open some of their wounds. The first that I touched was a case of frostbite. The toes of both the man's feet fell off with the bandages.'

It was for the want of Wellington boots after the victory at Inkerman that the overall battle was lost. W.H. Russell of *The Times*, the first objective war correspondent, wrote of the administrative incompetence over boots that made the British soldier a victim. His articles told of the sufferings endured by those who fought on the freezing uplands round the Russian fortress of Sebastopol.

'Hundreds of men had to go into the trenches at night with no covering but their greatcoats and no protection for their feet.' The troops, he said, were 'bare-footed, hopping about the camp, with the thermometer at twenty degrees and snow half a foot deep upon the ground'.

An immediate consequence of the disastrous Crimean War, which had been fought to shore up the crumbling Turkish Ottoman Empire ('the sick man of Europe'), was a dramatic improvement of British field hospitals. The Wellington boot by its tragic absence had been the unseen force that had started the revolution in army medical support.

Thereafter the boot continued to perform heroically at Rorke's Drift in the Anglo-Zulu War of 1879 and during the British annexation of the Transvaal Republic, which led to the First Boer War. Ironically the riding boot favoured by the Boers, who were essentially a guerrilla army in slouch hats with hunting rifles, was also the leather Wellington boot.

In 1881 Major-General Sir George Pomeroy Colley came across a Boer Force at Laing's Nek, a ridge that blocked the road four miles from the Transvaal border. The Boer force opened fire at the flanks of the 58th Infantry, who were marching up the open hillside in boots and red coats, carrying the colours before them. By the time the British attack was abandoned most of the regiment's officers were dead and their Wellington boots had been stolen.

The boot's military fate was finally confirmed after the siege of Khartoum, where General Gordon was killed and a subsequent dawn attack on the Dervishes at Ginniss was made to avenge his death. After victory at Ginniss the War Office decided that front-line British infantrymen would never again wear the red tunic into battle. Regiments were forced to change tunic, trousers and, sadly, the Wellington boot. By the time of the Siege of Mafeking, when Colonel Robert Baden-Powell, the author of *Scouting for Boys*, held out for 216 days, his soldiers – but not his officers – wore a drab tunic with short boots and puttees.

Years later, in an interview with the *Listener* magazine, the now Lord Baden-Powell explained how the Wellington boot had helped to teach him observation and deduction and inspired his book. 'I tracked down a thief by following his foot marks,' he explained. 'They were the foot marks of a soldier's boot, but not a Wellington boot, so I deduced that he was not a cavalryman but in the artillery.'

By the time the British Tommy went to France and Belgium in August 1914 he was a professional soldier who signed on for a minimum of seven years and was paid a shilling (5p) a day for his services. He wore khaki serge, puttees to protect his calves and short black boots. They were based on the old ankle-length 'Blücher' and made of pebble grain leather with steel nails. Officers wore a brown, lace-up leather top boot that reached to a height similar to the puttee.

The leather Wellington was now the preserve of the officer class. A boot of the type worn by

Stephen Fry in his role as General Melchett in *Blackadder Goes Forth* was sported by senior officers. The cavalry's riding boot could claim a close connection to the first Duke's footwear, and the archaic British and Indian Military Mounted Police still wore leather Wellingtons.

And, crucially, Lloyd George, Prime Minister of the coalition government in the second half of the war, saluted the original Welly's place in the Great War when he described General Douglas Haig, Commander-in-Chief of the British Expeditionary Force, as 'brilliant to the top of his Army boots'. Those boots were leather Wellington boots. In fact a group portrait by John Singer Sargent on display at the National Portrait Gallery shows that nearly all the First World War generals were conspicuous by their polished Wellies.

It was time for the cavalier leather Welly to make way for its sibling. This was a new century and it was the turn of the rubber Wellington to defend our shores.

Perhaps the best example of the new role that

the rubber Welly played, and was to come to play in the coming years, is its contribution to the famous 'Christmas Truce'. That truce, an event revered even by those who barely know the reasons for the outbreak of the First World War, has gone into legend.

A truce was not unique. In the Crimean War British and Russians had met for a smoke, and in the American Civil War Yankees and Rebels were said to have gone fishing together. But this truce was remarkable. On 25 December 1914 the English and the Germans scrambled out of their trenches on the Western Front, shook hands, exchanged gifts and played football. When the news reached Britain the newspapers, both local and national, ran scores of accounts of the extraordinary spell of peace.

The weather that winter was dreadful. 'The trenches are like rivers,' wrote Robert Scott MacAfie, colour quartermaster sergeant of the 10th King's Liverpool. 'We are having rainy weather – not at all pleasant to live in. Our legs are covered by Gum Boots from home.' ('Gum

Boot' was common slang for the rubber Wellingtons that were also known in cockney rhyming slang as 'daisies', after 'daisy roots'.)

And a letter from a lieutenant John Taylor of the 1st Royal Fusiliers, published in an Isle of Man newspaper in early January 1915, spoke of how those Gum Boots had played their part in that remarkable cease-fire. 'On Christmas Eve the Germans stopped firing and our chaps did the same. No firing was done that night and on Xmas Day our chaps, ready for sport, went over to the Germans and shook hands with them. We exchanged beer and cigarettes for wine and cigars and one of the Germans cut off all his buttons and gave them to one of our men in exchange for his pair of Gum Boots.'

The bartering of a Welly would not have surprised any Briton. The Wellington boot was an object of envy by the German soldier, and it soon came to represent more than just water-resistant footwear to the British. It personified our troops' more casual, amateur attitude to war.

'Our men in their scratch costumes of dirty, muddy khaki, with their assorted head-dresses of woollen helmets and battered hats, and their Gum Boots, are a light-hearted, open, humorous collection,' wrote Captain Mortimer in his jottings home. The Hun, on the other hand, he said, 'is of sombre demeanour and stolid appearance in grey-green faded uniforms, stiff top boots, and pork-pie hats'.

By October 1916 the rubber Wellington boot was regulation wear in the trenches, sanctioned by the 'winter scale'. This directive allowed the following articles of clothing to be worn in addition to ordinary service dress: waterproof cover for peaked cap, woollen drawers, woollen vest, worsted gloves, waistcoat, cardigan and Gum Boots 'as stocks allowed'. Everybody wanted a pair of Wellies – not for use in attack, as the boots could be sucked off in the mud, but to combat trench foot, which was rife.

A year earlier the War Office had commissioned the North British Rubber Company, still Britain's main manufacturer of the rubber Wellington boot, to construct a trench boot.

'The continued reports from the front of the

discomfort our brave defenders were suffering by standing in the trenches for hours on end in deep water and oozy mud, suggested to us that rubber might help to alleviate the discomfort and subsequent suffering,' the British Rubber Company reported disingenuously in its 1916 catalogue.

The company introduced four variations of rubber army boot, including a 'soft Wellington overboot' that was eighteen inches high with a strap and buckle around its top. It also sold a rubber trench sock and stepped up production of its classic vulcanised Wellington Boot, which it claimed was particularly popular with the military. 'Since the outbreak of the War those engaged in Naval or Military operations have found it necessary to include Rubber Wellington Boots in their kits,' it claimed. And by the end of the war it had manufactured almost two million pairs.

The Wellington boot had become the most important piece of kit to a First World War soldier. It was more than just another piece of regulation issue. It was of course an object of barter, it kept his feet warm and saved him from trench foot. But more vitally it put a smile on his face and helped him brave the hell of war. For it is during the Great War that the British started to laugh with, and at, the Welly.

The 1917 edition of *Blighty*, the magazine produced by and for the men at the front, refers to the game of 'Gum Boots and Craters'. The game played by the troops in the trenches involved throwing a Wellington into a set of designated shell holes, some of which were smaller than others. Scores were given according to the distance and difficulty of the hole. This jolly 'field sport' was the precursor to the English garden fête game now played across the globe and known as Welly Wanging.

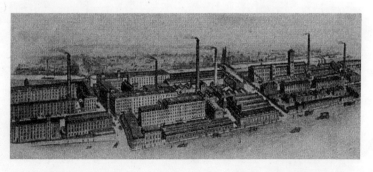

Demand for boots increased after the Great War

The Great War may have been the last hurrah for the leather Wellington but it also ushered in its rubber junior. The rubber Wellington boot was now both practical and a pastime – it stood proudly as a new patriotic symbol of Britishness.

At the end of the Great War the Avon Tyre Company, which along with North British Rubber had produced boots for the war effort, put a banner up in the grounds of its factory on the banks of the River Avon that quite justifiably read 'Victory Moved on Rubber'. The rubber Wellington had played a vital part in the war effort – as it was about to do once again in the world war still to come.

7

Welly's Finest Hour

The German jackboot—Stalin, son of a boot maker—
The Welly as Secret Weapon—The Welly digs for victory—
A Boot Amnesty—The Welly and nuclear war.

The Second World War was a pivotal moment in the history of the Welly. This was when the boot moved to the other foot. Welly fought against Welly; the rubber Wellington waged war on the home front, while the leather Wellington provided inspiration for the German army in the shape of the notorious jackboot.

The German soldier's Great War boot was a direct descendant, via the Franco-Prussian War, of the original leather Wellington boot. However, the marked difference from its illustrious British predecessor was that it was of heavier leather, with a thicker sole, and its upper was marginally higher at the front. It was the boot that was embraced early on by Adolf Hitler, who dressed his storm troops in it. Then it was known as the *Marschstiefel* (marching boot) and made from natural brown 'rough side out' leather. (Those early boots were blackened by the troops, as using black leather from the start would have made them 'too black', according to Lost Battalions, America's most accurate manufacturer of reproduction German uniforms.)

Slowly the boot evolved into a more menacing piece of footwear. The Nazi boot was a three-quarter-length boot with no toecap that was pulled on with a pair of black webbing straps sewn inside the uppers. Its soles were hobnailed, its heel was bound with metal and the bottom of the toe capped by screw-on metal plates. By the time it marched into Poland it bore little relation to the original Wellington boot that had graced the finest Victorian drawing-rooms.

The deadly precision with which these boots

were constructed is illustrated in the tragic story of Bombardier Alfred Jones.

Jones, from Aberavon, Port Talbot, followed the path of a lot of young men growing up in South Wales where work was scarce: he joined the army. He enlisted in the Royal Artillery aged seventeen and served mostly in India until September 1939 when he was sent to join the British Expeditionary Force in France, where he was captured. Although the Germans knew he was a soldier he was treated as a political prisoner and sent to Sachsenhausen (Oranienburg Concentration Camp, near Berlin). There he was used to test German military boots. He was one of several prisoners made to walk around a semi-circular track, which had different surfaces along it such as grass, asphalt and stones. Despite living on starvation rations he would be made to walk 25 kilometres a day carrying 30-pound packs on his back. If he faltered he was kicked and dogs were set upon him. There were occasional halts, but only to inspect the boots and make notes. In October 1944 Jones and the rest of the prisoners considered as dangerous to the State were transferred from Sachsenhausen to Mauthausen, in Austria. That was where he was sent to the gas chamber.

The boot that Jones was forced to test was the jackboot. It was effectively an armour-plated leather Wellington boot and it was to become a world-wide symbol of oppression.

All the Axis forces wore the German-style jackboot. So did the Russians. Joseph Stalin in particular loved his leather Wellies. The murderous dictator was the son of a boot maker who had worked as an apprentice in a Tbilisi shoe factory. Throughout his life he made a point of speaking to cobblers. In 1918 he commissioned a shoemaker in Tsaritsyn to construct an authoritarian pair of black Wellingtons to his specification. They were boots in which he would rule what was to become the USSR.

But the leather boot was not central to Britain's army uniform. Instead it capitalised on its more homely rubber Welly, which was to become its secret weapon.

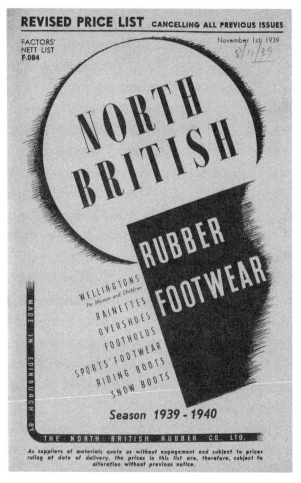

Wellington boots were central to the war effort

At the outbreak of war British Bata, the mass-production shoe company based at East Tilbury, had serious cash-flow problems and was about to go into receivership. The British government in its wisdom saved it by giving it huge contracts for Wellington boots and heavy-duty protective foot-wear. It did the same with the North British Rubber Company, which had done so much to help the troops in the Great War. Now it was contracted to produce Wellingtons not only for soldiers facing mud and wet but also for the home front as Britain had started to 'dig for victory'.

Rationing was introduced in early 1940, and the government ran a campaign calling for every man and woman to keep an allotment. Lawns and flowerbeds were turned into vegetable gardens. Chickens, rabbits, goats and pigs were reared in town gardens, and the Welly became an integral part of that effort.

In the winter, in the early days of the war, children and many adults wore Wellingtons because they were cheap and available. Many of those who worked on the land have fond memories of an early variation on a Ministry of Food advertisement, saying 'For the want of a nail . . . the battle was lost'. I remember hearing it as a child when my Aunt Dorothy, who had worked as a 'land girl', quoted it at me one wet day when I refused to put on my boots.

> Because of the Welly, the scraps were saved,
> Because of the scraps, the pigs were saved,
> Because of the pigs, the rations were saved,
> Because of the rations, the ships were saved,
> Because of the ships, the island was saved,
> Because of the island, the Empire was saved,
> And all because of the housewife's Welly.

Wellingtons were issued to anyone working on farms, in particular to the Women's Land Army. This was formed at the outbreak of war, when a thousand female volunteers were called upon to battle with the land and livestock. They were paid one pound eight shillings (£1.40p) a week for a fifty-hour minimum working week and wore a uniform of broad-brimmed khaki hats, green jumpers, brown jackets, corduroy breeches and

Wellington boots, which, it is frequently reported, they 'struggled to pull on and off'. By the end of the war the Land Army had swelled to 80,000 members, although by then many of them no longer had boots to work in. The war in southeast Asia had seen to that.

The Wickham seeds that had been so controversially transported from Brazil to Ceylon and Malaya over half a century earlier had by the first half of the twentieth century become the flower of the British Empire. By the 1940s the majority of Britain's rubber came from Malaya.

And so the Japanese invasion and subsequent occupation of the territory in 1941 was a fearful blow to the war effort. Not only did it affect the front-line fighting forces that used the material for a thousand purposes from tyres to groundsheets, but supplies for making boots for those fighting the less publicised war at home dried up completely. Soon Wellington boots were to be severely rationed.

It was a cruel blow. But the Welly was not about to surrender its position as the mainstay of the home front. The government started a poster and radio campaign to 'Make Do and Mend'. It encouraged people to repair their Wellingtons the best way they could, using cardboard or cork to cover the holes in the soles. There was even a much-advertised repair kit called Rhinosole to spread on the soles – although in truth it wasn't much good.

On the farms the Land Army was suffering from rheumatism because of the shortage of boots. In 1942 Derbyshire County War Agricultural Committee, for example, reported that it had only fifty pairs of boots to supply the whole county. In one district there were only ten pairs of Wellies to be shared between farms covering 80,000 acres of land.

'The workers are wearing ordinary shoes to work in the fields and are coming home with their feet soaking wet,' reported the *War Times*, complaining that there were boots hidden across the country. Organisations and individuals had been hoarding them, much as there were hoards of silk stockings and secret supplies of food.

The newspaper's editor, Evelyn Penn, thundered: 'Failure to provide reasonable protection for farm workers will put many people's health at risk. There are many rubber boots "standing by" in the country's ARP organisations. How many of them could be spared for essential farm work?' And the paper launched an advertising campaign to release those boots with the slogan 'Give Hitler the boot – and Give up your Wellingtons'.

Evacuees planting an apple tree at Elmbridge, Cranleigh, 1941

The campaign was a success. The Wellington boot was helping to win the war at home. But it still had one last battle – and this time it would come face to face with the jackbooted enemy abroad.

In December 1944 the German army halted its retreat and made a massive counter-attack in atrocious conditions against the Allied armies advancing into Belgium. It was known as the Battle of the Bulge, and the poor weather during the initial days of the offensive favoured the Germans because it grounded Allied aircraft. The British army was sent in to help extricate the Americans, and what it needed most was Wellington boots. This resulted in an immediate recall of all the Wellingtons issued to the Civil Defence.

Arthur Pay, a member of the Islington Civil Defence, remembers the moment well: 'As there seemed to be only a perfunctory control of the number of boots returned, some of the men in our squad thought it a good opportunity to "win" a pair of boots for themselves. But the police were waiting and searched our van when we returned to the depot.' The entire squad was 'bound over' by the local magistrate. There was no quarter given when it came to the serious matter of stealing Wellingtons that would save our boys at the sharp end.

Both at home and abroad the Welly had helped bring about victory. The Germans were routed, the Italians had surrendered and the victorious Stalin had given up his authoritarian boots. The Russian dictator had turned back to the *valenok* (the Russian word for a soft felt boot made from sheep's wool) because of the agony from his corns. He cut holes in the boots to relieve the pain and only wore the polished Welly when, according to Stalin's biographer Simon Sebag Montefiore, 'meetings with Winston Churchill required him to look the full part of a commander'.

Now the final battle for the boot appeared to be to help rebuild Britain's worn-out agricultural industry. There was an urgent need to reinvest in it, and among the measures of social reform introduced by Clement Attlee's new Labour government was the Agriculture Act of 1947. Among other provisions it guaranteed prices and markets, with the aim of ensuring the more efficient use of land. The recent memory of the war concentrated people's minds on the importance of self-sufficiency in food, and the boot was imperative to that effort. The Attlee government's intention was to make sure Britain never suffered a food shortage again and it therefore invested heavily in new farm equipment and rubber Wellington boots.

As it turned out the spectre of war did not depart for long, either for the nation or for the Welly. The Cold War was around the corner and the fear of a nuclear strike from Russia was beginning to worry the population.

Concerns over how to survive a nuclear winter came to a head in 1963 when the Cuban Missile Crisis brought the threat of nuclear war closer than ever before. Civil Defence plans had written off the chances of survival of those living in the immediate vicinity of an attack. Instead, the advice focused on improving the chances of those who were further away from the initial blasts.

An information booklet entitled *Protection Against Nuclear Attack* was published, containing advice for the public on how to survive an atomic war. It prompted one commentator at the time to write facetiously: 'The precautions for leaving the house after an H-bomb sound more like advice for a chilly day in the Home Counties, rather than the beginning of a nuclear winter.'

Be that as it may, the official line on how to cope with a nuclear holocaust wisely put its faith in a national icon. It read: 'If you have to go outside put on a hat or headscarf, coat done up to the neck, gloves and stout shoes or Wellington Boots.'

8

Green Welly

*The Welly sticks in the mud—The dawn of the green
Welly—Bespoke boots for a Princess—The Welly's return to
fashionable feet—The Sloane Hunter.*

The Second World War did no favours to
the Welly's image. The jackboot had
made stepping out in calf-high black
leather social suicide. The Duke of Wellington's
boot, worn by kings and potentates, soldiers,
sailors, dandies and thieves in scores of countries
across five continents for almost a century and a
half, was now a social pariah.

The boot had already disappeared from civilian
life, and even in the military it was now worn by
only a very few cavalry and guards regiments and
then only with their mess dress.

The change from leather to rubber had been

[107]

complete. And the rubber Welly, despite its wartime heroics, had metamorphosed into little more than a utilitarian rubber wader for the working man. It had, to put it brutally, become as common as muck.

Before the war the rubber Wellington boot was held in high affection by the upper classes. Both the county set and those who worked for them wore it. The style names given to the Welly in those days provide an indication of its standing. In the 1921 catalogue of the North British Rubber Company its men's Wellington boots were named 'Waterloo', 'Nelson' and 'Dreadnought' (and were sold in France under those names too). Women's Wellies were known as 'Queen', 'Empress' and 'Marchioness'. While for employees both male and female there was the all-purpose and somewhat cheaper 'staff' boot.

By the end of the Second World War, however, the Welly, which had been standard issue for many troops and played such a large part in civilian life, had become predominantly the workingman's friend.

This change was reflected by the more prosaic post-war Welly names – 'Greyfoot', 'Crag', 'Century' and 'Argyll'. The boot was now standard kit for manual labourers, while the pre-war ankle-length hobnail boot (with string tied around the trouser below the knee to prevent rats running up the leg) now looked dated and old-fashioned.

By far the biggest seller was the 'Argyll'. It was ubiquitous. Thanks to years of rationing, however, that boot with its thick sole and rounded toe was effectively the only choice. If you didn't buy the Argyll you were, to use an apposite expression, 'up a gum tree'.

Miners, dockers, navvies and council workers all wore it (and it is still produced to this day). There was barely a labouring man in the early Fifties who did not daily pull on a pair. Even Britain's champion ploughman John Gwilliam, who in a country starved of glamour was something of a celebrity, endorsed it. 'Farm work is tough on a boot,' said the winner of more than a hundred ploughing matches. 'Where I come from in Hereford the soil is heavy and clings to your boot, especially in wet weather. I must have a boot with a solid grip on muddy ground. It's Argyll for me all right!'

The advertisement made clear that the Wellington boot had picked itself up from the immediate post-war depression. But, like much in the early Fifties, what the boot really needed was a face-lift.

It still had one minor failing, a design fault that it had carried with it since its introduction in 1856 – it got stuck in the mud. In the ancient mudflows in the Dorset resort of Lyme Regis visitors can still find old Argyll Wellington boots that had to be abandoned when fossil hunters could not pull their boots out of the Jurassic quagmire. (Ben Green of Southam, Warwickshire, resolved the problem of the stuck Wellington some years later. Writing in the pages of the *New Scientist* he claimed: 'Wellingtons stick in the mud because an airtight seal forms around them. The simple solution is to securely attach a couple of vertical plastic tubes to the front and back of the boots, giving an air passage to the bottom of the boot and so preventing the seal from forming. The boots then lift easily from the mud.')

However, the black Argyll also stuck in the craw of the country's gentlemen farmers, gamekeepers and land agents who were enjoying a post-war agricultural boom. They wanted a dedicated field boot. They wanted a boot that was narrower and fitted better than the Argyll, one that did not get left behind on a stroll through ploughed earth. They wanted a boot that would hark back to the elegant leather Wellington, one to distinguish them from the urban labouring *hoi polloi*.

The firm which grasped this marketing opportunity was the North British Rubber Company. By the 1950s the company had moved from Edinburgh to the Heathall factory on the outskirts of Dumfries and was producing a range of 'industrial, agricultural and sea boot' Wellingtons. Most of them were from an identical mould. And just as Henry Ford is reputed to have made the statement that 'any customer can have a car painted any colour that he wants so long as it is black', so it was with the Welly.

The black boot was unquestionably popular – in 1954 eleven million pairs of them were produced in the UK alone by ten different manufacturers. But the boots were uninspiring. So much so that it might have gone the way of the bowler hat and the turn-up had it not been for the blue-sky thinking from North British Rubber. They came up with the ground-breaking idea of a green welly.

'There was a dream team at the North British factory then,' says Terry Sturgeon, a company stalwart who claims he was actually there in 1954 when the prototype boot was unveiled. 'The company knew there was a need for a purely agricultural boot. It had already decided on a name, Hunter, and had started to design it the year I joined.

'It was the time when, because of the war, everything was out of date. There was a mood for change. It wasn't the younger generation but the war generation that wanted something different from the great big wide Argyll Welly they had all been wearing for years. And that year a lot of research was done which reported to the company that the rural market was looking for something new.'

The 'dream team' of executives came up with the idea of a calf-shaped Wellington, a throwback to the original leather boot, that would eschew traditional black and be produced from green rubber. It was specifically designed for keepers and for those who shot and fished, and it would allow the wearer to keep his foot in the boot when it got stuck.

'In those days a green Wellington was revolutionary,' says Terry. 'That war generation was very conservative in the way it dressed. We had a lot of ice to break getting them into shops and we stuck our necks out.'

Unfortunately the boots didn't sell. The problem ironically was not that they were green but that the lasts used were the same as for the old black Argyll boot. 'Nobody was going to buy a green boot the same shape as the wide black boot just because it was green,' says Terry.

That first year, 1955, the company sold just

36 pairs. Not a single boot is known to have survived – they are Welly's own dodo.

Within eighteen months they acquired new lasts, designed and made from aluminium in Sweden in the same factory that made the first Aga stove, for two 'sporting' boots. One was the 'Hunter', a field boot 'with flexible net-lined leg and strap and buckle adjustment' in olive green, costing 41 shillings and ninepence (about £2.20). The other was the 'Stream fisher', an almost identical boot with a non-skid sole and a knee fastening that turned it into a wader. Both boots were considerably more expensive than the Argyll.

At first, as anticipated, it was keepers who wore them (after all it was keepers who pioneered waterproof boots fashioned from bullocks' bladders in the late nineteenth century). Then the grandees who shot and fished began to ape their skilled employees. And soon, through word of mouth, the feet of those who ran the estates of England were clad in the boot, including those of the Queen and the Duke of Edinburgh. The royal couple both wore Hunters. Special boots were then made for the keepers at Sandringham, and Hunters got the Royal warrant from both the Queen and the Duke.

The green Welly had taken the Wellington boot back into high society. The first Duke's boot once again trod the gravel of grand houses. The rubber boot that had so long been in the shadow of its leather parent was now its equal.

BY APPOINTMENT TO
HRH THE DUKE OF EDINBURGH
MANUFACTURERS OF WATERPROOF FOOTWEAR
THE GATES RUBBER CO. LTD.,
DUMFRIES SCOTLAND

Hunters (formerly the North British Rubber Company) hold the Royal Warrant from both the Queen and the Duke of Edinburgh

The result of this re-acquired status was a flurry of competition from the Hunter's rivals. Dunlop produced a series of 'seamless' Wellington boots for everything from rambling to riding motorcycles. A company called Dominion 'Heavy' Rubber Footwear introduced the 'Drifter' red fishing Wellington. Sperry began to make boots for sailing, and Nokia, now a successful mobile phone company, produced a stubby Scandinavian green Welly.

In the 1960s Uniroyal (the new name for the North British Rubber Company) produced an advertising poster claiming that it now produced 27 different varieties of Welly. They included the 'Cannery', a white half-Wellington for women workers in food factories, a 'Firesafe' with steel toe cap for firemen and the 'Oil Chief' for workers in the petroleum industry.

'You've got the job – we've got the boot' was Uniroyal's advertising slogan. And Admiral Gick, the naval hero from the Fifties, was featured praising its sea boot – 'a well designed boot for a well designed boat,' he said. It set the trend for 21st-century icons such as footballer Wayne Rooney to endorse footwear.

Terry Duckett, the sales manager of Gates' Rubber Company (the new name for Uniroyal), claims that its company's Wellingtons were used in Britain 'from birth to death'. Gates, he says, supplied 'white anti-static half-Wellington boots for surgeons in hospital delivery rooms and regular Wellington boots to councils across the country for gravediggers'.

The company even started making boots for cows and other animals. 'Modern cattle are more prone to foot infections and these are exacerbated by wet conditions underfoot,' says Duckett. 'The Wellington "hobbleboot" kit provides a tubular bandage and black boot designed to keep any dressing dry. Police dogs and sheep dogs, both of which get injured at work, are also fans of the hobble Welly.'

The sophisticated new Welly was soon a worldwide phenomenon. Canadians, for example, favoured black Wellingtons with red or green soles lined with warm insulating material. Ron

Bezant, from Ontario, remembers that when he was a child all the pupils wore Wellington boots. 'Some of us wore them all winter long with extra socks,' he said. 'The more fashion conscious of us folded the tops of them over. If we stepped into a hole the water would pour over the top of our boot and we'd get a soaker. But we also had to be careful in school. If we left them on during the day we could go blind. The teachers said so. Sort of like catching polio from running under the lawn sprinkler.'

In Alaska the brown and yellow Wellington boot, known as Extra Tufs, became so popular that they were worn with jeans to cocktail parties.

In Britain, however, it was the Hunter Wellington boot that was dominating the field sports, and in particular shooting, and was making the boot as socially acceptable as a Prada loafer.

Shooting always used to be the preserve of the upper classes. And it was organised with strict rules about what you shot, where you shot and what you wore to shoot. Tailcoats, waistcoats and leather Wellington boots were the outfit of the

Hunter Green Welly, universal symbol of Sloa-
nage from Land's End to John o' Groats, is fifty
this year. The preferred choice for the discerning
outdoor type, Hunter has, over the years, seen off
many rivals, maintaining a loyal fan base not so
much for the quality of the boot but for the social
cachet that the little red-rimmed label confers on
the wearer.

'Like all good British traditions there is a strict
and often idiosyncratic social hierarchy attached
to the wearing of Wellies. Farmers favour the
straightforward black variety. The 4 × 4 huntin'
shootin'n'fishin' brigade plump for the standard
green, the "Royal" hunter is favoured by those
with more money than sense. Boating types like
yellow Wellies, fashionistas like to experiment
with colour, while true toffs never wear green
Wellies, only black, as they'd much rather be
mistaken for the gardener than some lairy upstart
from the city.'

It had taken half a century, but the Welly no
longer had an image problem. It was back where
it belonged – on the feet of the moneyed.

9

Welly à la Mode

Bloomers and Wellingtons—Gertrude Bells steps forth—The Welly in Swinging London—Poka-dotted, striped and animal-printed Wellingtons—Moss in Boots.

In the winter of 1850–51 American reformer Amelia Bloomer wrote an article in *The Lily*, her New York temperance newspaper, condemning the restrictive clothing worn by women. She advocated that women should wear a sensible coat-like frock worn over trousers that would be tucked into soft leather Wellington boots.

The idea was not a universal success. The *New York Tribune* laughed and labelled her trousers 'bloomers'. The subsequent ridicule forced her and her fellow American campaigners for emancipation such as Susan B. Anthony and Elizabeth Cady Stanton, to make a swift return to traditional long dresses, petticoats and elastic-sided ankle boots.

In Britain the public and press treated the idea with equal disdain. The *World of Fashion* magazine described Amelia Bloomer's new way of dressing as no more than a cover for 'women's rights' and teased it as 'manly and commanding'.

Yet this early appearance of the bloomer and Wellington boot was evidence of the first stirrings of the movement towards female emancipation that by 1888 saw playwright Oscar Wilde's wife Constance editing the radical *Rational Dress Society's Gazette*. The magazine, which ran for six issues, wanted to get rid of 'the discomfort and impracticality of contemporary fashion for women' and demanded the wearing of sensible, practical clothes and boots.

'She [fashion] extends her authority to the minute details of our lives,' it complained. 'She tells us when we must eat and when we must strive to amuse ourselves. She turns day into night, ignores our comforts, disposes of our money and our time, and engages in successful war even with Nature itself.'

This radical idea was not only supported by other free-thinking journals including the *Women's Penny Paper*, and *Woman's Signal* but also by the boot-wearing Oscar. In an article on 'woman's dress', one of his shorter prose pieces, he complained about the hoops and crinolines of the day while advocating the wearing of Wellington boots. 'Soft leather boots, which could be worn above or below the knee, are more supple, and give consequently more freedom,' he wrote.

The Wellington boot, after losing its fashionable standing in the mid 1850s, was now being saluted by the great playwright and, what was more important, by the modern woman. But it was still a daring concept in dress for women. It was little more than an unattainable dream, and remained so until the Great War, when women's fashion finally began to change. Skirts rose, trousers were slowly to become acceptable and, thanks in part to Gertrude Bell, the creator of modern Iraq, the Wellington did at last deservedly become a female fashion item.

Bell, a slim woman who usually dressed in billowing muslins, was the daughter of a wealthy northern coal magnate. She was the first woman to obtain a first-class degree in modern history from Oxford University (in 1888) and subsequently became an archaeologist, a linguist and the greatest woman mountaineer of her age. She also travelled alone through the Arab world with a camel-train carrying her formal English clothes. 'By Allah! what must the men be like?' said an awed Arab dignitary.

During the war she worked for the British government in the Middle East and was responsible for ensuring that the state of Mesopotamia (Iraq) was founded from the Ottoman provinces of Mosul, Baghdad and Basra. At that time she spoke fondly of her Wellies. In a letter from Iraq to her father in February 1917 she writes: 'We have had five days of rain and Basra is a unique spectacle. It's almost impossible to go out. I put on a riding skirt and a fine pair of India Rubber Wellington boots – which I had fortunately procured from India – and stagger through the swamp for half an hour after tea.'

Her acknowledgement, however tiny, that she wore rubber Wellies in public was one of a number of sartorial victories for women that stemmed from the uprising started by Amelia Bloomer. It was a movement that would ultimately lead to the future Princess of Wales stepping out with her Prince in Wellies.

The first mass-produced rubber Wellington boot that came off the production line in 1856 was unquestionably a macho bit of kit. The North British Rubber Company did not consider women in its early plans to shoe the Western world in rubber. And in the following years despite scores of developments and patents – one of which was taken out for 'improvement in the manufacture of Wellington boots', with only the legs made of rubber – it remained staunchly male and with little fashion sense. In the illustrated catalogue of 1886 issued by Bloomingdale's, New York's most famous department store, there is no mention of Wellingtons or rubber boots for women. And despite a 1902 prediction in *India Rubber World* that in the next century 'the shapes of rubber boots will lose their masculine appearance' (a statement prompted by the newly patented zip) there was no sign of change. In fact London's Army & Navy

Stores catalogue for 1907 did offer one style of black glazed rubber Wellington boot (at nine shillings) – for women below stairs.

It was not until the mid 1920s, after Gertrude Bell and others had proved that it was acceptable for women to wear Wellies, that the Rubber Grower's Association would write glowingly of its feminine style boots in its 1928 promotional booklet *Rubber and the Home*. 'Rubber footwear to-day is produced in a variety of attractive styles to meet every conceivable purpose,' it reported. 'The transition from crude waterproof shells to Wellingtons in all their variety has happened overnight.'

The writer then proceeded to wax lyrical: 'The full length knee Wellingtons which are very easily slipped on and off are a veritable armour against cold and chill and are now produced in extraordinarily attractive styles and have achieved enormous popularity. Rain and slush, snow-covered streets or mud-covered fields hold no fears for those who wear rubber Wellingtons. Neither damp nor cold can penetrate this sensible footwear which is an admirable protection against wet feet and legs and saves many chills and doctors' bills. High boots in coloured rubber – saxe blue, beige and rose – are the latest novelty in rubber footwear.'

The eccentric reason given for this rise in popularity of the women's boot was, according to the Association, that 'hard pavements make walking noisy and jar the head while rubber makes walking a pleasure'. They may have had a point. Within thirty years Greta Garbo would be seen on the streets of New York in her rubber Wellington boots. The *Daily News* carried a report of the actress strolling anonymously along Beekman Place on the East side of Manhattan in headscarf, dark glasses and calf-length rubber boots.

Unfortunately the Second World War halted the march of the fashionable Welly. Crude rubber was stuck in the East and Wellingtons returned to the colonial catalogues as conservative as ever. It was more than a generation before the boots recovered as a mode item. However when they did, they did so with a baby-boom bang.

In the summer of 1964, less than a year after the assassination of President Kennedy, the Beatles made their first tour of the USA and launched a British cultural invasion. The lovable mop-tops from Liverpool popularised three distinct styles: long hair, the crew-neck Beatle jacket and the elastic-sided chisel-toed black Chelsea boot. The hair caught on, the jacket did not. As for the boots, which had evolved from a mid-nineteenth century Victorian boot that in turn was a bastardised and shortened version of the first Duke's Wellington, they have never gone out of fashion.

On the back of the Beatles' success Mary Quant launched her mini-skirt. This kicked off 'Swinging London' after a fashion show held on board the *Queen Elizabeth* cruise liner in 1965, and she then took thirty outfits to the USA, where the models in their thigh-high dresses stopped traffic in New York's Times Square. That year she also introduced her famous cosmetics range with its daisy logo and launched the wet-look vinyl boot. It was fashionably cut around the calf, high-heeled and unquestionably based on the leather Wellington boot.

Before the 1960s fashion had been aimed at a

wealthy, mature élite, and at the beginning of the decade it was still dominated by Parisian designers of expensive *haute couture* garments. They included André Courrèges, who opened his 'Maison de Courrèges' in the Avenue Kléber in Paris in 1961. Early in the decade he broke from the classic *haute couture* mould and began turning out simplistic clothes including, in 1964, the mini-skirt and the shift dress. It was the year he created his 'Moon Girl' look, a flared mini-dress with plastic portholes complemented by a low-heeled, calf-high boot made of four pieces of white plastic and ornamented with a clear cut-out slot near the top. It was the original 'Wellington boot' in all but name and material. Only the heels at the bottom and the plastic slot at the top distinguished it from its illustrious leather predecessor. It was quickly embraced and bastardised by a host of designers, including Quant. She admits she took the idea for her boot from the 1964 Courrèges designs and, liking the shorter styles, she made the boots even shorter for her boutique Bazaar. She is rightly credited with popularising the high-heeled PVC Welly, which now holds pride of place at the Northampton Shoe Museum.

As Swinging London took hold, so did the groovy new boots. They tramped the streets of cities world-wide, and that year Nancy Sinatra sang about them with her single 'These Boots are Made for Walking', a song that subsequently sold four million copies.

At first the boots that Mary made and Nancy sang about were nameless. To call them 'tight Wellingtons' would have muddled them up with the rubber boots worn by labourers and been ludicrously 'uncool'. Fortunately an old Ealing comedy inadvertently came to the rescue.

In 1941 the SS *Politician* sank off the Scottish Island of Eriskay, and eight years later the film *Whisky Galore* recounted the story of how the locals raced to retrieve the ship's liquid cargo and hide the bottles of Scotch before the excise men could find them. A few years after the release of the film a Parisian café owner renamed his bar after the title of the film – the direct translation into French being 'Whiskey à Gogo'. A decade later a club owner in

Washington DC had the novel idea of having caged women dancers jiggling about in mini-skirts and the Courrèges/Quant boots, and he borrowed the Parisian name. The disco on Capitol Hill inspired Smokey Robinson and the Miracles' 1966 hit 'Going to a Gogo'. And it was from that song that the new tight-fitting Wellington boot took its name – to become the 'go-go boot'.

Honor Blackman and Diana Rigg wore the boots in the TV series *The Avengers*. (Patrick Macnee and his co-star Blackman even composed a song entitled 'Kinky Boots'.) The original *Star Trek* series had the female officers wearing regulation go-go boots, and in 1966 they were worn by the cheerleaders for the inaugural season of the Miami Dolphins.

Soon the skirts got shorter and the boots went higher. In 1970 Quant introduced hot pants worn with floor-length maxi-coats, which swung open to reveal go-go boots. And Barbara Hulanicki's trendy shop Biba, whose first premises were an old chemist's shop in Kensington Church Street, popularised the natural successor to Quant's wet-look boot, the knee-high suede boot. Biba also produced a successful collection of old-style, well-cut rubber Wellington boots in glittering colours considered so outré by the 'now' generation that they were worn as ordinary city boots and out clubbing to some of London's hottest venues such as the Embassy. The boots are still revered. The author's father His Honour Judge Quentin Edwards continues to wear his electric blue Biba gumboots when gardening.

The go-go boots' sudden rise in the Sixties left the Welly it had been cloned from in the dustbin of fashion. But the Wellington boot was not to be spurned. In the Seventies it began to establish itself as a fashion item in its own right.

It first reappeared as part of the counter-culture when Californian artist Eleanor Antin started to photograph a hundred Wellington boots in different situations. She sent her pictures of '100 Boots' as postcards to friends. There were '100 Boots go to war', '. . . in a field', '. . . on a ferry,' . . . crossing Herald Square', '. . . facing the sea' and so forth. She claimed the boots were 'culture icons'. The postcards were eventually bought by and displayed in the New York Museum of Modern Art in 1973. At the time one critic spoke for all when he said the show 'powerfully evokes the America of the Vietnam Era'. In the foreword to the book of the collected postcards, Henry Sayre of Oregon State University claims that '100 Boots' is more than just photographs of pairs of boots, it is a political statement. He suggests it is an integral part of the anti-Vietnam war movement: 'It is as if 100 boots are announcing their solidarity with Abbie Hoffman and Rennie Davies, members of the "Chicago Seven" who were arrested for conspiring to disrupt the government.'

And then, like much from the counter-culture, Wellington boots began to move into mainstream fashion.

In the Seventies the rubber boot aficionado could buy two-tone Wellingtons for golf, heeled boots made by Nokia, and Wellies with a pin-heel from Dunlop. The Welly was slowly beginning to capture a new market. By the Nineties the 'good old-fashioned welly' (as it is always disparagingly referred to by women's magazines) was at last a high fashion item. In 1994 Chanel retailed a black pair of Wellington boots based on the old Argyll with a pair of interlocking 'C's on the vamp at £250. The highly respected Suzy Menkes, the fashion doyenne of the *International Herald Tribune*, described them as 'the latest must-have accessory'. The following year, 1995, it was Gucci's turn and the Italian fashion house produced a pair with its distinctive snaffle logo at a more reasonable £165. Thomas Pink, the Jermyn Street shirt makers, started to sell pairs in a particularly lurid pink to female punters at £35.00 to tie in with its sponsorship of National Hunt Racing at Cheltenham. Finally in 2003 Burberry produced its pair of plastic (rather than rubber) Wellingtons. They were immediately copied and sold cheaply at local markets the length of breadth of the country. It had taken two centuries for the elegant, high-fashion Wellington boot to filter down to the mass-market fashion of the Chav.

It was at this point that fashion guru Paul Smith

realised that the Wellington boot was more than just a season's gimmick for the fashion houses. Smith encouraged Tamara Henriques to mass-produce the boot, then still considered by many in the trade as a joke, as a genuine designer item.

Henriques is now the reigning queen of the fashion Wellington boot. 'I decided to design rubber boots for a very simple reason,' she says. 'I grew up in Scotland, where I lived in Wellington boots. When I moved to Hong Kong, where it rains non-stop for months at a time, it dawned on me: why are these boots only available in army green? And wearing flip-flops in puddles was definitely not the answer.'

She sold her first pair of floral boots to Paul Smith. British *Vogue* photographed them and described them as 'this month's must-haves'. The fashion Welly business was born. Within months she was selling to Europe, the USA, Canada and Japan. Those early prints have now bloomed into stripes, polka dots, paisley, plaids, hearts and animal prints. She has even produced a Wellington cowboy boot.

'Rebellious and oh so sassy mid-calf rubber boots in true Paul Smith style! The pointy toe and sexy pink kitten heel make these eye-catching and fabulously fun boots both rain and big-night-out appropriate!' is how her Wellington boots were described. And they can be seen in capitals across the wet Western world.

But it is not just the designer Welly that is sported like stilettos. In 2005 Britain's most cele-brated beauty Kate Moss made her fashion state-ment on the front page of every newspaper by combining a pair of Hunter Wellington boots with a gold mini-skirt at the Glastonbury Festival. It turned the Welly boot into the apogee of cool. And Kate was not alone. Actresses Gwyneth Paltrow and Keira Knightley, soul singer Joss Stone and the rest of female Cool Britannia paraded their sassy independence in Wellington boots.

The Welly had made it as a must-have female fashion accessory – Amelia Bloomer and her pioneering cohorts would have been proud of it.

Welly Oblige

*Pink Wellingtons in Dumfries—The fiftieth anniversary of
the Green Wellington—To PVC or not to PVC?—
Wellington's final word.*

The early squalls from the damaging gales
that swept over Carlisle and south-eastern
Scotland also lashed the outside of
the former Heathall car factory in Dumfriesshire
– the first purpose-built pre-stressed concrete
building to be built in Scotland. Inside the
dim, hot and noisy machine room the handful
of half-naked manual labourers remained impervious
to the wrath of nature. They were too busy
wrestling with large lumps of pink bubblegum of
the sort and size that the Jolly Green Giant might
find stuck to the bottom of his over-sized shoe.

The men were pushing the tacky substance on

to giant rollers which, as the air was expelled, popped with the suddenness of burst balloons before emerging the other side as flat and as oblong as a jumbo stick of Wrigley's. The chewy material then moved inexorably along a production line where it was cut into shape, wrapped around a last by hand, racked up and baked at 130°C in an oven the size of a ship's boiler.

The rack finally emerged to reveal, sitting in neat upside-down rows, a hundred pairs of vulcanised shocking pink Hunter Wellington boots waiting to protect the great and the good and anybody else with fifty quid from the gathering storm in the Solway Firth.

The Hunter Rubber Company (the firm was now named after its most famous boot) produced these blushing Wellingtons in 2005 in aid of the Haven Trust. A percentage of the profits from every pair went towards the breast cancer charity. The boot was such a success that it crossed the Atlantic to star in the *Oprah Winfrey Show*, the most successful chat show in the USA.

Hunter also produced boots in half a dozen

other jolly colours, each representing a different charity that would subsequently profit from the shade.

The reason for the Scottish boot company's philanthropy was to celebrate a very British birthday – the fiftieth anniversary of the Green Wellington Boot. It was not an anniversary that Hunter could ignore. Fifty years ago the black Welly sat between dog worming powders and chicken wire in the local country retail outlet, as anonymous as pink baling twine and paraffin. But the creation of the green Welly in 1954 began the restoration of the boot to its rightful place in history as progeny of a Duke.

Nowadays it is the aristocrat that 'does its bit'. The sophisticated Smartie-coloured boots are merely the tip of the iceberg with regard to its hard work raising money and public awareness for good causes. The Welly is a stalwart of the charity circuit, suffering daily the indignity of being thrown at fêtes, signed by celebrities and auctioned, as well as walking sponsorship miles and running in marathons.

And when it is not involved in worthy work it sits on the shelves in Sloane Street, Harrods, Harvey Nichols and on Fifth Avenue as a silent advertisement for all that is best in Britain. It is at the cutting edge of the carriage trade bracketed with such classics as the Purdey shotgun, the Savile Row tweed suit and the Range Rover.

Today there are four main producers of the top-of-the-range Wellington boot, and owing to its burgeoning popularity they include foreign companies. Claude Chamot, an agricultural engineer from Cherbourg, created Chameau boots in 1927. It now has its headquarters based in a Normandy château. Aigle is a modern French company sited on a former US Army base, with roots in walking-boot manufacture. In the USA the Original Muck Boot Company started up in Rock Island, Illinois, in 1999, whereas the Hunter Rubber Company is the direct descendant of the 1856 North British Rubber Company. All four companies can claim to make a Wellington boot of which the grand old Duke would have been proud.

'Wellingtons are emerging from the post-war years, when they were thought of as the lowliest of all clothing, as top-of-the-range goods,' said Malcolm Harris, the owner of The Welly Shop, in Ross-on-Wye, Britain's first dedicated Wellington boot outlet. 'Nowadays the best Wellington boots are at the best end of the retail market. They are zipped and lined with leather and can be worn comfortably for almost any activity one can think of.'

This re-emergence of the well-made Welly for the urban backwoodsman and the rural sophisticate has been achieved in the face of competition from the PVC boot, known in the trade as 'Cheap'n'Chinese'.

Polyvinyl chloride (PVC) was discovered late in the nineteenth century when scientists found that the gas vinyl chloride turned into a solid lump when it was exposed to sunlight. That lump was ignored until the 1920s, when rubber for Wellingtons was becoming ever more costly. American scientists then set to work to develop an alternative cheaper synthetic rubber, and PVC was the result.

Ironically it was not the boot that benefited from the discovery or immediately turned PVC into a household name, but the stocking. Wallace Carothers, one of the scientists struggling with vinyl material, discovered the silky PVC in 1935 when he pulled a heated rod from a jar containing a mixture of the new molecules. Two years later Du Pont patented that material. It was shown at the 1939 World Trade Fair in New York, under a name based on abbreviations of New York and London, the cities where its development had taken place. By Christmas that year 64 million pairs of nylon stockings had been sold. (And the tornado that carried Dorothy to the Emerald City in *The Wizard of Oz* was also made from the wonder material.) The search for a cheap boot had produced a cheap stocking.

By the end of the war, with rubber in short supply, it was not just the stocking trade that was benefiting from PVC. There was an explosion in the use of it. It was cheap to produce and could be used to make hundreds of products, from insulating cable, plugs and sockets to sewage pipes and golf balls. But among all the thousands of objects available in PVC it was the bastardised Wellington boot that gave the material its glamour.

For Mary Quant and Courrèges used PVC to make their wet-look Wellies. And it was those early PVC boots that led to the fetish boot scene, which the British pop artist Allen Jones exploited in his paintings and sculptures. The PVC boot soon became as much part of the modern sex industry as the plastic vibrator.

Meanwhile the classic Wellington boot was copied in PVC. The moulded plastic Wellington was easy to manufacture and easily patterned. It was a pale imitation of the real thing, but the Welly, like Cartier watches and Louis Vuitton leather goods, was ripe for rip-off.

China now produces the boots by the tens of millions, and other Third World countries have followed suit. Even Dunlop, once the most advanced rubber-processing company in England, but long since split up into hundreds of different companies, is knocking them out. Its boot company is now owned by the Dutch giant Hevea and produces three million Wellington boots annually from its factory in Portugal. 'The modern equipment in the polyurethane factories, with its impressive computer control systems, robots and high formulation accuracy, looks more like an orbiting satellite than a Wellington boot production unit,' boasts its publicity bumf.

The elaborate words hide the fact that the PVC boot is a shadow of its rubber original. The PVC Wellington boot may have become a world-wide phenomenon – but like all cheap imitations its value has been debased.

In China the boots have become the mark of the peasant, and nobody who earns more than five pounds a month would dream of wearing them. German workers wear them reluctantly because in that country the boots have a reputation for being smelly. They are worn by aid workers in the Third World as a crude alternative to vaccines as a means of preventing the spread of diseases, while the British have turned the great Wellington boot into childish frog-eyed boots and vulgar fake leopard-skin footwear.

The PVC boot has become so ubiquitous that a French television channel was induced to make a documentary on the importance of the PVC Wellington boot in the modern world. The PVC Welly has become footwear's Big Mac.

And yet despite this PVC onslaught the classic rubber boot survives. In New Zealand, for example, single farmers wear 'Red Stripe' boots, the equivalent of the old Argyll boot, to display their earning power, while in Sweden they love the old-fashioned Welly so much that the boots have become day-to-day office wear.

'Rubber is an all natural product,' says former Hunter Rubber Company managing director Mark Sater. 'An all rubber boot is as natural as an all leather shoe. There are none of the synthetic materials favoured by the average Wellington boot manufacturer. The raw material comes from the best trees that depend on good soil and the right balance between sunlight and rainfall. There is nothing unnatural in the rubber production. And when the boot is worn out it will eventually return organically back to earth.'

Hunter's ecologically friendly rubber Wellington boot is now so sophisticated that it is latex-dipped on the last and, after passing through 28 pairs of hands, can rightfully claim to 'fit like a glove'.

'Until the Green Hunter the rubber Wellington boot was little more than an ill-fitting cover for your feet,' says Mark Sater with a cavalier disregard for its history. 'There was a misinformed view as to how accurate the cut of a rubber boot could be. Hunter discovered the rubber boot can be cut incredibly accurately. The rubber boot is still miles ahead of today's clever one-piece moulded PVC boots. Little else comes close in comfort or fit.'

Except, that is, for the £300 Hunter 'Crown' Wellington made from leather (with a rubber sole). Almost two centuries after its birth, the leather Wellington boot has returned. And its appearance prompted the eighth Duke of Wellington to write to the company to ask for a pair.

The Duke is one of the few living Englishmen to have owned two pairs of leather Wellingtons of original design. When he joined the army in 1938 he had a patent leather pair that he wore with mess dress under 'overalls' (the tight trouser with a strap under the instep that is indistinguishable from the trousers worn by his great-great-great-great grandfather). He also had a regular pair of polished leather worn with Full Dress. Now he wanted a new pair of ancestral boots.

The first Duke could never have dreamed that his great-great-great-great-grandson would lust after his casually designed boots – quite the reverse in fact. For what he thought of as mere boot bagatelle, a frippery that had emerged from the serious business of defending his country from a marauding French emperor, would eventually eclipse any of his achievements.

In the winter of 1849 there was a meeting between the Duke of Wellington and Lord Brougham. Henry Brougham, a lawyer, politician and Lord Chancellor of England, lived at the heart of intellectual life in Victorian Britain and counted the Duke of Wellington as one of his closest friends. In the 1820s Brougham helped to create the University of London and to provide libraries for workingmen. He was a passionate supporter of the abolition of slavery, brought about radical reform of the British legal system and was responsible for popularising the French city of Nice and the naming of its seafront as La Promenade des Anglais. Among his many other talents he designed a horse-drawn carriage with a low coupé body, with a box seat for the driver and one forward-facing seat for two passengers. His manservant nicknamed it a 'Brougham'. It was such a successful carriage that when Cadillac, the American car manufacturer, was looking for a classy name for its 1916 model it plumped for 'Cadillac Brougham'. The company revived the name in 1957 when it unveiled the chrome and fin 'Cadillac Eldorado Brougham' known as the 'Cadillac of Cadillacs'. It was more expensive than the comparable Rolls-Royce of the day, was driven by stars such as Little Richard and Chuck Berry, and later itself starred in films, from *Driving Miss Daisy* to *Get Carter* and *Grease*.

A late-nineteenth-century report of the meeting between Wellington and Brougham reads as follows:

> Lord Brougham had driven to the House of Lords in a vehicle of his own invention, which Robinson the coachmaker has christened after him, when he was met in the Robing Room by the Duke of Wellington, who after a low bow, accosted him.
>
> *Wellington*: 'I have always hitherto lived under the impression that your lordship will go down to posterity as the great apostle of education, the emancipator of the Negro, the reformer of the law, but no – you will hereafter be known as the inventor of the carriage.'
>
> *Brougham*: 'And, my lord Duke, I had always been under the delusion that your grace would be remembered as the hero of a hundred battles, the liberator of Europe, the conqueror of Napoleon, but no – your grace will be known as the inventor of a pair of boots.'
>
> *Wellington*: 'Damn the boots, I had forgotten them – you have the best of it.'

But Brougham hadn't. The footwear invented by the Grand Duke as a matter of convenience so that it could be worn comfortably under trousers, has left its mark on the history of the modern world more indelibly that the great man himself.

The British may think of Waterloo as our greatest victory, but the winning commander's boot should hold equal ranking in our collective memory. It is the boot of Empire, of the Wild West and the Far East, of the trenches and the dig for victory and now of the trendy, the charitable and the global village.

And yet, for all its grandeur, it remains an object without pretensions. And perhaps it should be left to comedian Billy Connolly, in his memorable song, to sum up the worth of the Welly.

> If it was nae for your wellies where'd you be
> You'd be in the hospital or infirmary
> 'Cause you would have a dose of the flu or
>   even pleurisy
> If you did nae have your feet in your wellies.

With Thanks To
Mark Sater and Amanda Sater
For their support of this book.

Index

[156]

Index

Index

Index

Index

Index

Index